Abdullah al-Udhari was born in Taiz, Yemen, in 1941, and has lived in London since 1962. He studied classical Arab literature and Sabaean epigraphy at London University, where he also received a doctorate for his pioneering study, *Jahili Poetry before Imru al-Qais 4000 BCE–500 CE,* which established him as an authority on early Jahili literature. He is a literary historian, poet and storyteller, and the author of *Voice Without Passport, The Arab Creation Myth* and *Modern Poetry of the Arab World.* He is also editor of *Victims of a Map: A Bilingual Anthology of Arabic Poetry* (also by Saqi Books).

First published in 1999 by Saqi Books

This paperback edition published in 2017

ISBN 978-0-86356-047-7

A full CIP record for this book is available from the British Library.

Printed and bound by Clays Ltd, Elcograf S.p.A

Saqi Books
26 Westbourne Grove
London W2 5RH
www.saqibooks.com

Classical Poems by
Arab Women

Edited by Abdullah al-Udhari

SAQI

Laura

1
One morning Allah visited the earth but the sun was not in sight.

2
Allah said: 'The earth is still dark?'

3
And He created you.

لَوْرَا

١

ذَاتَ صَبَاحٍ زَارَ اللهُ الأَرْضَ والشَّمسُ لا تُرَى.

٢

قال اللهُ: "لا تَزَالُ الأَرْضُ مُظْلِمَة؟"

٣

فخلقكِ

'The Prophet Muhammad, bless him, said: "Do not approach your women like animals, but establish a link between you."

They said: "Rasulullah, what is this link?"

He said: "The kiss."'

Hadith

1

What shall I do, my love's coldshouldered me and plucked sleep from my eyes?

2

He won't even grace me with a glance, so I leave him to Allah, Who knows what he's up to.

San'ani Folk Poem

Morning star, you've seen me waiting for him, now that he's back he's reading the Qur'an.

San'ani Folk Poem

قال الرسول "ص":

"لا ترتموا على نسائكم كالبهائم، بل اجعلوا

بينكم وبينهن رسولا".

قيل: "وما الرسول يا رسول الله؟"

قال: "القبلة"

حديث

ما حيلتي والخِلّ قد جَفَاني

وشَلّ نوم العينْ وابتلاني

ما زِدْ تتازل لي ولا بنظره

أمره الى الله، هُوْ عليمُ بسرّهْ

قصيدة صنعانية تراثية

واشهَدْ عليه يا نجمْ يا مِغَلِسْ

فِتَحْ لي الخِتِمِة وقام يدْرِسْ

قصيدة صنعانية تراثية

Contents

The Andalus Period (711-1492)

Introduction

I
Women's Poetry

Classical Poems by Arab Women takes a new look at classical Arab poetry and differs from the standard perception of Arab poetry in three ways. Firstly, it pushes back the starting date from 500 CE to 4000 BCE. Secondly, it tells the story of Arab poetry through women's eyes. Thirdly, it shows sharply focused snaps of the world of men lensed by women.

The standard history of classical Arab poetry begins and ends with a man, with the odd woman thrown in, who is either tearing her eyes out over the dead or tantalizing men's desire with song and lute. Women poets appear as incidentals and the biographical dictionaries devote minimal space to them, in spite of the fact that their contribution to the growth of the literary tradition is as significant as that of the men.

Women poets have been around since the earliest times, yet their diwans (collected poems) were not given the same attention as the men's, even though the women poets may have been princesses, noblewomen or saints. Apart from Khansa's diwan, no other diwans by women have yet appeared. A number of anthologies of women's poems were edited in the Abbasid and later periods, but only two or three anthologies have been published, though in mutilated form. Contemporary editors, unlike the openminded classical anthologists, some of whom were respected theologians such as Suyuti (1445–1505), assumed the role of society's moral guardians and abused the integrity of the texts.

II
The Veiling and Walling of Women

Arab society had a relaxed approach to sex. In the Jahiliyya a woman had complete freedom to marry or go with any man of her choice. Although polygamy was practised, it was up to the woman to agree to join a polygamous household, and if she was not happy with her husband's treatment she had the right to divorce him at will. Also, a woman could have as many boyfriends as she liked, and if she bore a child, she was the one who decided whom to name as the father, and the man concerned had to accept his paternal responsibility, even if he was not the biological father. On the other hand, if a brothel woman conceived, it was left to the client to acknowledge the paternity of the child since he had paid for her services. Similarly, the child of a concubine was legitimized only after the master's paternal acknowledgement.

After the establishment of Islam, the women's privileges were transferred to the men. The process of women containment was started by the Prophet Muhammad, who invariably invoked Allah for revelationary support to justify his hold on women. His constant recourse to revelationary back up provoked his wife Aa'isha to tease him: 'Your Lord is always on call to endorse your whims.' But as women in early Islam were still imbued with the Jahili free spirit, the Prophet could not fully put the stopper on women's free will.

In Umayyad and Abbasid societies men and women mixed freely in mosques, taverns, markets, streets and their own homes. Lovers met openly in their favourite haunts, and society ladies drew both sexes to their salons. The Prophet's greatgrand daughter Sukaina bint al-Husain (d. 735) and Aa'isha bint Talha (d. 719) vied with each other in attracting to their salons the leading poets, composers, singers, scholars and pleasure seekers of their day. Sukaina and Aa'isha even defied their jealous husbands by refusing to wear the veil, saying Allah had made them beautiful for all to see. The husbands divorced Sukaina and Aa'isha, who married again without having to suffer the indignity of wearing the veil.

Umayyad and Abbasid men were not stcuk up about their womenfolk's sexual needs. When Ulayya bint Al-Mahdi expressed her love for some of her slaves and was gossiped about, her brother the Caliph Harun Arrashid (766–809) chastised her for not being discreet about her love affairs and forbade her for a while to mention the names of her slavelovers in her poems. Further, Ulayya's father, the Caliph Mahdi (744–785), used his wife, Khaizaran, to procure for him the wives of his officials and beneficiaries in order to deprive his followers of their honour and break their will. Mahdi's husbandbreaking policy is called *diyatha*, and is still flourishing in the Arab world as a politically effective taming tool.

By the end of the Abbasid period women had almost lost their freedom. And after Tamerlane's sacking of Damascus and the rape of the Damascene women by his hordes in the mosques in the presence of their menfolk in 1400, the need to protect women became urgent. In consequence, women lost their freedom and their world was finally veiled and walled by of their menfolk. The veiling and walling of the women pleased Arab rulers as it neutralized half of

Arab society and made it easier for them to sheep the other, male half.

In Andalus it was a different story. Since Andalus was separated from Mecca, Medina, Jerusalem and Baghdad by the Mediterranean Sea, any attempt by these centres to shout down Andalusian women with religiopolitical bigotry was drowned in the Mediterranean waters. As a result the Andalusian women disregarded socioreligious taboos and asserted their independence by living their lives as they pleased and writing openly about their own world. In many ways the Andalusian women retained the free spirit of the Jahili women.

III
The History of Women's Poetry

In spite of two hundred years of Arabist scholarship, the history of Arab poetry has yet to be written, because there are no definitive editions of the work of any poet nor comprehensive studies of poets or periods. All the existing studies of Arab poetry are generalizations based on rehashed and unstudied opinions.

In the case of women poetry the fewness of the existing poems makes it almost impossible to draw a full picture of the history of women poetry. On the other hand, *Classical Poems by Arab Women* presents a sketch of the history of women poetry for the first time and includes poems from the first five periods, namely the Jahiliyya, Islam, Umayyad, Abbasid and Andalusian.

The Jahiliyya (4000 BCE–622 CE)

Arab tradition traces the origins of the Arabs and their language to the end of the Nuh (Noah) Flood. The story goes that when Nuh and his eighty passengers came out of the Ark and built the town of Thamanin (eighty) they all spoke one language. One night the eighty passengers were visited in a dream by the angel Jibreel (Gabriel) who taught each of them to speak a different language, and only Nuh could communicate with all of them. One of the passengers was a man by the name of Jurhum who was taught to speak Arabiyya (the Arab language). Jurhum was the ancestor of the first Arab people known as the First or Early Jurhumis, who later perished without a trace.

Another tradition traces the origins of the Arabs to the Wind of Babil incident. Tradition relates that when the population of Thamanin outgrew the town the people moved out to another area and built the town of Babil (Babylon) within an area of sixty square kilometres. As time went by the Babilis grew to a hundred thousand people who spoke one language and were dominated by seventytwo families. The seventytwo families decided to build a Mijdal (castle), which was two thousand five hundred metres high and one thousand five hundred metres wide, to protect them from disease and floods. Allah was not pleased with the seventytwo families for embarking on a project He had not sanctioned. So He ordered Jibreel to summon the North Wind, the South Wind, the East Wind and the West Wind to destroy the Mijdal, blow each of the seventytwo families on to a different road and to teach each family to speak a different language. One of the languages Jibreel taught was Arabiyya. The Aribiyya speaking family ended up in Yemen and some of their descendants were the people of Aad, who lived around 4000 BCE.

Arab tradition has preserved a collection of poems from the Aad period, of which the poem by Mahd al-Aadiyya is a fine specimen. The poem, which is the earliest example of a *muzdawaj* (heroic couplet) form, warns the Aadis in vivid and dramatic imagery of their impending doom because they preferred to worship their gods instead of Allah:

I see people riding on shrieking horses,
steering clouds of sparkbelching fires
on their way to flame life out of you.

Another Jahili people who trace their descent to the Aad period were the Tasmis and the Jadisis who, before their demise in the third century CE, lived in Bahrain and were ruled by the Tasmi king, Imliq. Imliq was a notoriously despotic king whose excesses involved the raping of the Jadisi brides on their wedding nights. When Afira, the daughter of the Jadisi king, was raped on her wedding night by Imliq, she was outraged by her people's acceptance of their humiliation. She railed at them in two poems, which stirred them to rage, and ultimately led to the extermination of the Tasmi king and his people as well as the Jadisis. Afira's first poem is a *muzdawaj* in which she lambasts the Jadisis:

No one can be as low as the Jadisis who
watch the rape of their brides.

And in the second poem she enthuses them:

Spark the fire of war and kill the tyrant
or be killed, or take to the wilderness
and starve, for it's better to die honourably
than live in shame.

Laila bint Lukaiz (d. 483), one of the leading poets of the fifth century, was in love with her cousin Barraq ibn Rawhan (d. 470), but was promised to a Yemeni prince. When Laila was on her way to Yemen to marry the Yemeni prince, she was kidnapped by a Persian prince who locked her up in his castle for scorning his advances. Laila appealed to Barraq and her brothers to save her and assured them:

> The foreigner lies, he never touched me
> and I am still pure, and I'd rather die
> than share his bed . . .

The poem whipped up the courage and moral fervour of her people and led to her successful rescue.

The Basus War that started in about 494 between the Bakris and the Taghlibis and raged for forty years produced some of the greatest war-obsessed poems in the Jahiliyya. One of the best Basus War poets was Jalila bint Murra (d. 540) who describes her shock as a victim caught in the web of a war triggered by murder:

> My womenfolk, today time has catastrophed
> me and encircled me with fire, since crying
> for a day or two is not like crying for an
> untomorrowed day.

Khansa (d. 646) is the only woman poet to have attracted the attention of the classical editors and critics, who regarded her as the greatest Arab woman poet. Most of her poems are elegies on her dead brothers and sons killed in the Jahiliyya and the Islam wars. Her poem on the death of her brother Sakhr, killed in the Jahiliyya, is memorable:

> The rising and setting of the sun keep
> turning on my memory of Sakhr's death . . .

The Islam Period (622-661)

The Jahiliyya ended in 622 when the Prophet Muhammad (571-632) moved out of Mecca to Medina, where he set up his Muslim government and launched his offensive against the enemies of Islam. In 631 he took Mecca and made it the capital of the new Islam state. The Prophet was succeeded by the Caliphs Abu Bakr (573–634), Umar (584–644) and Uthman (577–656) respectively. The socalled fourth caliph, Ali (600–661), the cousin and soninlaw of the Prophet, was not a fully confirmed caliph because, unlike the previous caliphs, he failed to get the unanimous *bay'a* (power endorsement) of the faithful required to qualify for the caliphate.

Most of the women's poems of this period are conventional elegies. The anonymous poem about the wife complaining to the Caliph Umar about her husband, who neglected his marital duties by spending most of his time in the mosque, is an exception:

> Judge of sensible verdicts, the mosque has
> kept my man away from me.

The Umayyad Period (661–750)

The death of the Islam Caliph Uthman in 656 triggered a sixyear civil war, during which Mu'awiya ibn Abu Sufyan (603–680), the governor of Syria and Ali's rival, succeeded in winning the unanimous *bay'a* and establishing the Umayyad caliphate in 661 with himself as the first caliph.

The Umayyads ruled from Damascus and extended the borders of the Arab empire to the borders of China in the east and to Andalus (Iberian peninsula) in the west. Mecca and Medina became the liveliest cities of their day, and the haunts of funlovers.

Laila bint Sa'd (d. 688) was the love of the poet Qais ibn al-Mulawah (d. 688), better known as Majnun Laila. While Majnun celebrated his love for Laila in the most passionate poems in the Arab language, Laila had to bear the burning stings of love's fire silently. Laila's selfcontrol, unlike Majnun's selfpity, is indicative of the Umayyad women's intellectual and moral strength:

> I have been through what Majnun went through,
> but he declaimed his love and I treasured mine ...

One of the most striking poets of the Umayyad period is Maisun bint Bahdal (d. 700), the wife of the Caliph Mu'awiya. Maisun was a countrywoman who hated urban life, and her description of the contrast between town and country is delightful and has a touch of humanity born out of loneliness. The depiction of her caliph husband as 'a bloated foreign mass' and her preference for her 'finefigured cousin' emphasizes the independent spirit of the Umayyad women. Laila al-Akhyaliyya (d. 709) is considered by classical critics as the Umayyad Khansa, though her poems are conventional. She was attached to the court of Hajjaj ibn Yusuf (660–714), the governor of Iraq and the Eastern provinces, and was the object of unconsummated passion of the poet Tawba ibn Humayyar:

> I have a friend I will not betray, so
> stick to your mate.

The Abbasid Period (750–1258)

The Abbasids overthrew the Umayyads in 750, and their authority covered the whole of the Umayyad domain except Andalus, which remained under Umayyad sway after an Umayyad escapee made it to Andalus and strengthened his family's control over it in 756. During the Abbasid rule, whose capital was Baghdad, the Arabs reached the peak of their political, economic and cultural influence. Economic prosperity, the socially liberal nature of the caliphs and the questioning of socioreligious taboos helped create a society bent on enjoying Allah's earthly gifts to the full. By the time of the Caliph Mutawakkil (821–861), who boasted of mating with all his three thousand concubines, the concubines began to have a say in directing the reins of power. As the caliphs were the offspring of concubines, the caliphs' mothers took an interest in the political welfare of their sons. And this in turn led to the rise of concubine power, which dominated the Abbasid court until its demise in 1258. Incidentally, of the thirtyseven Abbasid caliphs, thirtyfive were the offspring of concubines.

Historians regard the Abbasid period from the Caliph Mahdi to the Caliph Harun Arrashid as the 'Golden Age' of Arab civilization. But the poem of Hajna bint Nusaib tells a different story. The poem cuts through the 'Golden Age' gloss to show the reality of the underprivileged majority of the Abbasids:

> Hardship has drained our strength and there's
> no one to bail us out, yet the scented pools
> of the generous caliph are full.

A major figure in the history of sufism is Raabi'a al-Adwiyya (714–801) whose concept of divine love:

I love You a double love: I love You
passionately and I love You for Yourself ...

set the route for sufi successors to walk on and raise their signposts along the
way. Her obsession with Allah left no room in her heart and mind for love for
any person, not even the Prophet Muhammad. What is surprising is that, despite
Raabi'a's prominence, her diwan has not been preserved.

Ulayya bint al-Mahdi (777–825) was the Caliph Harun Arrashid's favourite
sister on account of her songs, lute playing and wit. When Harun forbade her
to mention the names of her slavelovers in her poems, she confessed to Allah:

Lord of the Unknown, I have hidden the name
I desire in a poem like a treasure in a pocket.

The carefree nature of Abbasid society is reflected in a lighthearted poem
by Juml (ninth century), who takes to task her decrepit master, the poet Idris
ibn Abu Hafsa:

Juml, if you had been a good Muslim,
Allah wouldn't have lumbered you with
a youthless pile like Idris, whose
spenturge is time's worst joke on you.

The idea of marriage was not the dream of all Abbasid women. This is
evident from the poem of Zabba bint Umair ibn al-Muwarriq (ninth century):

I will not be a husband's claim, so shame on the
two angels if they don't write: 'It's better to
live in hardship than ending up as a whipping girl.'

The Andalusian (Iberian) Period (711–1492)

In 711 Tariq ibn Ziyad (670–720) led the Arab army from Morocco across the
Pillars of Hercules into the southern part of the Iberian peninsula, and waited
for his commander Musa ibn Nusair (640–715) to follow him, and together
they completed the conquest of Iberia within a short space of time. In honour
of Tariq the Pillars of Hercules were renamed Jabal Tariq (Gibraltar).

The Arabs called the Iberian peninsula Andalus and its people Andalusians, irrespective of whether they were from what later came to be known as Spain or Portugal. But since the start of Arabist scholarship in the nineteenth century, scholars have perceived the Andalusian civilization as essentially Spanish, overlooking its Portuguese orientation. It is time the Arabists removed their Spanish blinkers to have a full view of the Andalusian landscape that runs across Spain and Portugal, and acknowledge Portugal's role in moulding the Andalusian heritage.

The Arabs turned Andalus into 'paradise on earth' and translated the Qur'an's paradisial world into their own world and revelled in it. For this reason the people of Cordova, Seville, Silves and Lisbon saw themselves as paradisians rather than earthlings, and made sure they enjoyed the unrestricted paradisial pleasures.

The first Andalusian women poets began to make their presence felt in the ninth century. The poetry of this century was mainly derivative. The tenth century witnessed the emergence of women poets whose work reflected their Andalusian carefree world unperturbed by the taboos that eventually stifled their sisters on the eastern wing of the empire.

Hafsa bint Hamdun, who lived in the tenth century, is one of the first distinct voices to embody the Andalusian women's will to speak their mind and challenge the arrogance of muscle power. When her lover boasted that she 'couldn't have had a better man,' she hit back, 'Do you know of a better woman?'

In the eleventh century a number of women poets thrived, and the most famous was Wallada (d. 1091), the daughter of the Umayyad Caliph Mustakfi (976–1025). She was the love of the poet and vizier Ibn Zaidun (1004–1071). Wallada's relationship with Ibn Zaidun was not always smooth, especially when she felt he was betraying her:

If you were faithful to our love you wouldn't
have lost your head over my maid.

Sometimes she was merciless in lashing out at Ibn Zaidun, calling him a sexobsessed homosexual:

If he saw a joystick dangling from a palm tree
he'd fly after it like a craving bird.

Ashshilbiyya was a twelfthcentury poet from Shilb (Silves) in southern Portugal. She was a determined woman who championed the cause of her abused people and strongly reminded the Almohad Sultan Ya'qub al-Mansur (1160–1199) of his responsibility to his Shilban people:

Tell the emir when you reach his door:
'Shepherd, your flocks are dying and have
nowhere to graze. You left them as prey
for the raiding beasts.'

Hafsa bint al-Hajj (d. 1190), a noble lady from Granada, was in love with the poet and vizier Abu Ja'far ibn Sa'id (d. 1163). Hafsa's love for Abu Ja'far was no secret, as he was the centre of her life:

If I keep you in my eyes until the world
blows up I'd still want you more.

The above historical sketch gives an indication of the power and range of women's poetry, and reveals that women's wit is far more subtle than men's predictable humour. Women, therefore, are not the vain and manipulative creatures men have been portraying through the ages, but the equal of men, if not superior to them.

1
When women tell you not to touch them they mean get on with it.

2
They promise you hell and stick to their word, but when they promise you heaven they fool you about.

3
Women are like trees, some are edible, others sourish.

Ubaidallah ibn Qais Arruqayyat (633–694)

IV
Voicecopy Poems

Classical Poems by Arab Women is a collection of poems in Arabiyya and English. The English poems are the voicecopy of the Arab poems and vice versa. The English and Arab poems speak the same thoughts, express the same emotions and mirror the same colours, but flow distinctly to reflect the different climates under which they were written. The Arab poems flow in their own set pattern, while the English poems flow in their new paraline (paragraph line) form.

The Arab poems represent the undying spirit of the timetraveller, who stops at a given time and place, and leaves English poems as mementos of his stopover before moving on.

Now let us listen to the women telling their storypoems and discover a humanity blurred by a manmade veil.

The Jahiliyya

(4000 BCE–622 CE)

Mahd al-Aadiyya (4000 BCE)

Mahd was an Aadi whose people clashed with Allah over whom they should worship. The Aadis worshipped seventy gods while Allah wanted them to worship Him as the One and Only God. The Aadis told Allah they were happy with their gods and would not bow to His Will. Allah sent the Aadis His prophet Hud to warn them of His wrath, but they mocked Allah's threats and snubbed His prophet. Allah was furious and plagued the land of Aad with drought that starved the Aadis and their animals. The Aadis sent a delegation to the Ka'ba to pray for rain. The delegation feasted for a month before their Meccan hosts reminded them of their mission. In the Ka'ba Allah showed the delegation a white cloud, a red cloud and a black cloud, and asked them to choose one of the three clouds, which would then be sent to their land. The delegation chose the black cloud, thinking it was the rainiest of the three clouds. Allah told the delegation they had chosen the cloud of fire and destruction. The black cloud sailed to the land of Aad and scorched the land and its people, and only the prophet Hud and his followers were spared.

When Mahd spotted the black cloud approaching the land of Aad she warned her people:

1
I see people riding on shrieking horses, steering clouds of sparkbelching fires on their way to flame life out of you.

2
So believe in Allah, the One and Only God, and hold on to Hud, the prophet of the One and Only worshipped Lord, to save yourselves, for doom is soon coming to finish you off.

مهد العادية

تنثر من ضرامها الشرارا	إني أرى وسط السحاب ناراً
تهتف بالأصوات والصهيل	يسوقها قوم على خيول
فوحدوا الله لكي ما تسلموا	وهي عذاب يا آل عادٍ فاعلموا
نبيّ ربٍّ واحد معبود	ثم استجيروا بالنبي هُودِ
فليس تبقي منكمُ من باقية	فقد أتاكم عن قريب داهية

Afira bint Abbad (third century CE)

Afira was also known as Ashshamus.

In the third century CE Yamama (Bahrain) was inhabited by the Tasmi and Jadisi peoples, who trace their descent to the Aad period and were ruled by the Tasmi king. A Jadisi couple had a disagreement over the custody of their child and appealed to the Tasmi king to resolve their problem. The king's verdict was that the couple should be sold as slaves and one fifth of the woman's price should be given to the man, and one tenth of the man's price should be given to the woman and their child should join the king's household as a slave. The couple were unhappy with the outcome and the woman complained about the king's injustice. The king reacted by forcing each Jadisi bride to spend her wedding night with him. As the Jadisis were weak they agreed to the king's demand until Afira, the daughter of the Jadisi king, got married to her cousin and had to go through the same fate as other Jadisi brides. After Afira spent her wedding night with the Tasmi king, she came out of the palace, tore the front part of her wedding dress, which was stained with her virginal blood, and declaimed two of the most powerfully indicting poems in the Arab language. The two poems stirred the anger of her people. So her brother invited the Tasmi king and his nobles to dinner, and while the Tasmis were enjoying their meal the Jadisi hosts pounced on them and killed them all. Then they turned on the rest of the Tasmis and killed everyone except the Tasmi poet Riyah ibn Murra who escaped and sought the help of the Himyari king, Hassaan ibn Tubba. King Hassaan promised Riyah to avenge the death of the Tasmis, and set out with his army to punish the Jadisis. Riyah warned King Hassaan of the exceptional eyesight of his sister Zarqa al-Yamama (the blueeyed girl of Bahrain), who was married to a Jadisi. Riyah suggested to the king that bushes and trees be cut and used to camouflage his soldiers' approach to the Jadisi stronghold. Zarqa spotted the camouflaged soldiers advancing from a distance of three days' march and warned the Jadisis of the coming danger in the form of moving bushes and trees, but they ignored her warning. King Hassaan surprised the Jadisis and wiped them all out. As for Zarqa, King Hassaan was curious to know what made her eyesight powerful, so he gouged out her eyes and found that her eye veins were black. He asked her why they were black, and she said she used kohl on her eyes.

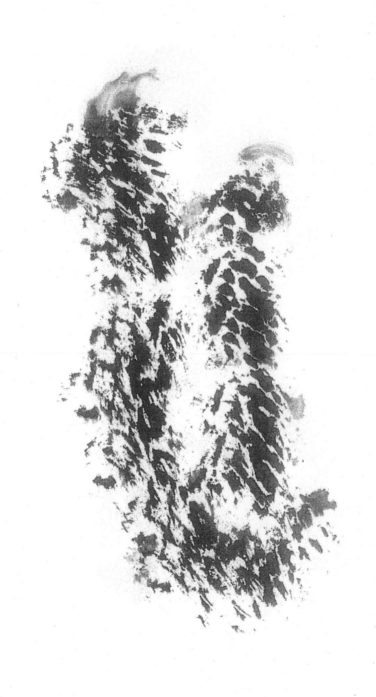

~❀~

1

No one can be as low as the Jadisis who watch the rape of their brides.

2

How can a freeborn groom who's given his gifts and dowry put up with this sting?

3

He should take his own life than see his bride done in.

عَفِيرة بنت عَبَّاد

أَهَكَذَا يُفْعَلُ بالعَرُوسِ	لا أحد أَذَل من جَديسِ
أَهْدَى وقد أَعْطَى وَسيقَ المَهْرُ	يَرْضَى بهذا يا لَقَوْمِي حُرُّ
خيرُ مِنْ أَنْ يُفْعَل ذَا بِعِرْسِهِ	لأَخْذَةُ الموتِ كذا لنفسِهِ

1

What's become of you that you let the king rape your brides?

2

You are as numerous as the ants, yet Afira walks in broad daylight stained with her virginal blood.

3

If we were men and you were women we'd stop this crime.

4

Spark the fire of war and kill the tyrant or be killed, or take to the wilderness and starve, for it's better to die honourably than live in shame.

5

But if you're not moved by this outrage, you might as well bathe in scent and kohl your eyes and wear the bridal dress.

6

Death to cowards who strut like men among women.

وَأَنْتُمْ رِجَالٌ فِيكمُ عَدَدُ النَّمْلِ   أَيَجْمُلُ مَا يُؤتَى إِلَى فَتَيَاتِكُمْ

جِهَاراً وَزُفَّتْ فِي النِّسَاء إِلَى بَعْلِ   وَتُصْبِحُ تَمْشِي فِي الدَّمَاء عَقِيرَةٌ

نِسَاءً لَكنَّا لاَ نُقِرُّ بِذَا الفِعْلِ   وَلَوْ أَنَّنَا كُنَّا رِجَالاً وَكنْتُمُ

ودبُّوا لِنَارِ الحَرْبِ بالحَطَبِ الجَزْلِ   فَمُوتُوا كِرَاماً أَوْ أَمِيتُوا عَدُوَّكُمْ

إِلَى بَلَدٍ قَفْرٍ وَمُوتُوا مِنَ الهُزْلِ   وَإلاَّ فَخَلُّوا بَطْنَهَا وَتَحَمَّلُوا

وَلَلْمَوْتُ خَيْرٌ مِنْ مُقَامٍ عَلَى الذُّلِّ   فَلَلْبَيْنُ خَيْرٌ مِنْ مُقَامٍ عَلَى أَذَى

فَكُونُوا نِسَاءً لاَ تُعَابُ مِنَ الكُحْلِ   وَإِنْ أَنْتُمُ لَمْ تَغْضَبُوا بَعْدَ هَذِهِ

خُلِقْتُمْ لأَثوَابِ العَرُوسِ وللغِسْلِ   وَدُونَكُمُ طِيبَ العَرُوسِ فَإنَّمَا

وَيَخْتَالُ يَمْشِي بَيْنَنَا مِشْيَةَ الفَحْلِ   فَبُعْداً وَسُحْقاً للَّذِي لَيْسَ دَافِعاً

Laila bint Lukaiz (d. 483)

Laila was in love with her cousin the poet Barraq ibn Rawhan (d. 470), but she was promised to a Yemeni prince who was the patron of Barraq. While Laila was on her way to Yemen to marry the Yemeni prince, a Persian prince who had failed to win her hand in marriage had her kidnapped with the help of Bard al-Iyadi and the Anmaris. After the Persian prince tried to win Laila's love and failed, he locked her up in his castle. Laila sent the following poem to Barraq and her brothers urging them to rescue her. Barraq rallied his people and marched to the Persian castle and freed her.

The Iyadis and the Anmaris trace their descent to the patriarch Iyad ibn Nizar (fifth century BCE) and Anmar ibn Nizar (fifth century BCE).

Adnan (seventh–sixth centuries BCE) is the great patriarch of the northern Arabs and was killed in Nebuchadnezzar's wars when Nebuchadnezzar (king of Babylon 605–562 BCE) swept across northern Arabia on his way to Jerusalem in 586 BCE. Adnan was the greatgrand father of the patriarchs Iyad, Anmar, Rabi'a and Mudar who was the ancestor of the Prophet Muhammad.

The Taghlibis were Laila's people, who traced their descent to the patriarch Rabi'a ibn Nizar (fifth century BCE).

1
I wish Barraq had eyes to see the painful state I'm in.

2
Kulaib, Uqail, Junaid, damn you brothers, I'm your sister, help me out.

3
The foreigner lies, he never touched me and I'm still pure, and I'd rather die than share his bed.

4
It was you, bastard Anmaris and Iyadis, who told the Persian fool where to find me, but my will broke your deal, and Bard the sneak who traded me in went blind with shock.

5
Banu A'mas, don't cut the Banu Adnan's rope of hope, and if we hold our ground victory will spring out of despair.

لَيْلَى بنت لُكيز

ما أُقاسِي من بَلاءٍ وعَنَا

لَيتَ للبرّاقِ عَيناً فَتَرَى

يا جُنَيْداً ساعِدُونِي بالبُكَا

يا كُلَيْباً، يا عُقَيْلاً إخوتي

بِعَذابِ النُّكرِ صُبْحاً ومَسَا

عُذّبَت أُخْتُكُمُ يا ويلَكُمْ

معي بعضُ حِساساتِ الحَيَا

يَكْذِبُ الأَعْجَمُ ما يَقْرُبُني

كُلَّ ما شِئتُمْ جميعاً من بَلا

قَيَـــدُوني غَلِّلُوني وافعَلُوا

ومَريرُ المَوْتِ عندي قد حَلاَ

فأَنَا كارِهَة بُغْيَتِكُمْ

يا بَني أَنْمَارَ يا أَهلَ الخَنَا

أتَدُلُّونَ علينا فارساً

ورَمَى المَنْظَرَ مِنْ بَردِ العَمَى

يا إيَادُ خَسِرتْ صَفْقَتُكُمْ

لبني عدنانَ أسْبابَ الرَّجَا

يَا بَني الأَعْمَاصِ إمَّا تَقْطَعُوا

كلُّ نَصرٍ بعد ضَرٍّ يُرْتَجَى

فاصْطِبَاراً وعَزاءً حَسَنَا

6

Tell the Banu Adnan I give my life for them.

7

Now rally your men and fly your flags and wave your swords, and in the sunlight glare march to the Persian lines, and your grit will turn the battle.

8

Be alert and ready, O Banu Taghlib, and don't let shame scar your lives, your sons and the memory of your people.

لِبَني الأعْجَامِ تَشْميرَ الوَحَى	قُلْ لَعَدْنَانٍ فِدِيتُمْ شَمِّرُوا
واشْهَرُوا البِيضَ وسِيرُ في الضُّحَى	واعْقِدُوا الرَّايَاتِ في أَقْطَارِهَا
وذَرُوا الغَفْلَةَ عنكمْ والكَرَى	يا بَني تَغْلِبَ سِيرُوا وانْصُرُوا
وعليكمْ ما بَقِيتُمْ في الوَرَى	واحْذَرُوا العارَ على أَعْقَابِكُمْ

Jalila bint Murra (d. 540)

Jalila was the sister of Jassas (d. 534) and the wife of the poet Kulaib (d. 494), the despotic king of the Taghlibi and Bakri peoples. Jassas's aunt Basus had a camel called Saraab that strayed into Kulaib's land. Kulaib, a Bakri, who had warned his subjects he would kill any animal trespassing on his land, killed Saraab. Basus, a Taghlibi, was incensed by the killing of Saraab and urged her nephew Jassas to kill Kulaib. Jassas killed Kulaib and Kulaib's death caused the Basus War between the Taghlibis and the Bakris, which lasted forty years. Jalila, who was a Taghlibi, moved back to her father's home.

Jalila wrote the following poem in response to Kulaib's sister, who accused her of being involved in the murder of her husband.

1
Noble lady, don't be so quick to throw your blame on me, first unhusk the facts, then lash on.

2
If the sister of the murdered lashes at me out of grief, so be it.

3
Jassas's killing act weighs me down, the regret pain of what has been done and is to be done has left me in shreds.

4
Jassas's killing act, though I love him, broke my back and pushed me to death.

5
If an outsider had snuffed the light out of my eye I wouldn't have cared, for the eye puts up with the fraternal stings like a mother bearing the hurtful pranks of her child.

6
Your death, husband, brought down the roof over my head, and my brother destroyed the house I've just built and turned to undo my old home.

7
His death struck me like a man shot at close range.

جَليلة بنتُ مُرَّة

يَا ابْنَةَ الأَقْوَامِ إِنْ لُمْتِ فَلاَ   تَعْجَلِي بِاللَّوْمِ حَتَّى تَسْأَلِي

فَإِذَا أَنْتِ تَبَيَّنْتِ الَّذِي   يُوجِبُ اللَّوْمَ، فَلُومِي وَاعْذُلِي

إِنْ تَكُنْ أُخْتُ امْرِئٍ لَيْسَتْ عَلَى   شَفَقٍ مِنْهَا عَلَيْهِ فَافْعَلِي

جَلَّ عِنْدِي فِعْلُ جَسَّاسٍ فَيَا   حَسْرَتِي عَمَّا انْجَلَى أَوْ يَنْجَلِي

فِعْلُ جَسَّاسٍ عَلَى وَجْدِي بِهِ   قَاطِعٌ ظَهْرِي وَمُدْنٍ أَجَلِي

لَوْ بِعَيْنٍ فُقِئَتْ عَيْنِي سِوَى   أُخْتِهَا فَانْفَقَأَتْ لَمْ أَحْفِلِ

تَحْمِلُ الْعَيْنُ أَذَى الْعَيْنِ كَمَا   تَحْمِلُ الأُمُّ أَذَى مَا تَقْتَلِي

يَا قَتِيلاً قَوَّضَ الدَّهْرُ بِهِ   سَقْفَ بَيْتَيَّ جَمِيعاً مِنْ عَلِ

هَدَمَ الْبَيْتَ الَّذِي اسْتَحْدَثْتُهُ   وَانْـــثَنَى فِي هَدْمِ بَيْتِي الأَوَّلِ

وَرَمَانِي قَتْلُهُ مِنْ كَثَبٍ   رَمْيَةَ الْمُصْمِى بِهِ الْمُسْتَأْصِلِ

8

My womenfolk, today time has catastrophed me and encircled me with fire, since crying for a day or two is not like crying for an untomorrowed day.

9

The avenger cools his fire with revenge, but my revenge triggers more grief.

10

I wish my blood could be a ransom for my husband's death.

11

I am the killer and the killed, may Allah save me from this curse.

يَا نِسَائِي دُونَكُنَّ اليَوْمَ قَدْ   خَصَّنِي الدَّهْرُ بِرُزْءٍ مُعْضِلِ

خَصَّنِي قَتْلُ كُلَيْبٍ بِلَظَىً   مِنْ وَرَائِي وَلَظَىً مِنْ أَسْقَلِي

لَيْسَ مَنْ يَبْكِي لِيَوْمَيْنِ كَمَنْ   إِنَّمَا يَبْكِي لِيَوْمٍ يَنْجَلِي

يَشْتَفِي المُدْرِكُ بِالثَّأْرِ وَفِي   دَرَكِي ثَأْرِي نُكْلُ المُثْكِلِ

لَيْتَهُ كَانَ دَمِي فَاحْتَلَبُوا   دِرَراً مِنْهُ دَمِي مِنْ أَكْحَلِي

إِنَّنِي قَاتِلَةٌ مَقْتُولَة   وَلَعَلَّ اللهُ أَنْ يَرْتَاحَ لِي

Umama bint Kulaib

Umama was the daughter of Kulaib (d. 494), the king of the Rabi'a people, whose murder triggered the Basus War. As soon as her father was killed by his brotherinlaw Jassas and his cousin Amr, she went to her paternal uncle, the poet Muhalhil, and was upset to see him drunk and blurted out at him:

1

You waste your time on the bottle and pleasuring about, oblivious to what goes on.

2

You're not aware treacherous Jassas and Amr had killed Kulaib and dared to do the uncommittable.

3

To hell with Jassas and Amr who lunged your brother with scorpioned spears.

4

Get up and pull the spears out of your brother's corpse, for no one defies us and gets away with it.

أُمَامَة بنت كُلَيب

ولا تدري بعاقبة الأمور	أتلهو بالملاهي والخمور
قتيلاً عند جساس الغدور	ولا تدري بأن كليب أضحى
لقد جسرا على أمر نكير	فواعجبا لجساس وعمرو
لقد رميا أخاك بعنــقفير	ويا ويلاً لجساس وعمرو
فما أحد علينا بالجسور	فبادر وانزعنَّ الرمحَ منه

Safiyya bint Khalid al-Bahiliyya

Nothing is known about the poet but the poem was written on the death of her brother according to some sources, or on the death of her husband according to other sources.

1
We were twin shoots sprouting beautifully on a tree.

2
When our branches spread, our shade stretched and our buds flushed, time snapped my other shoot.

صفية بنت خالد الباهلية

كنا كغصنين في جُرْثُومَةٍ سَمَقَا

حيناً بأحْسَنِ مَا يَسْمُو لَهُ الشَّجَرُ

حتى إذا قيل قد طَالَتْ فُروُعُهُمَا

وطَاب فيآهُمَا واستُنْظِرَ الثَّمرُ

أَخْنَى على واحدي رَيْبُ الزَّمَانِ

وما يُبْقِي الزمانُ عَلَى شيء لا يَذَرُ

Juhaifa Addibabiyya

Nothing is known about the poet.

1
What a man you gave me, Lord of all givers.

2
He's a nasty old lump of wrinkles with shrivelled fingerbones and a bent back like a croaking crow.

جُحَيْفَة الضِّبَابية

وَهَبْتَهُ وَأَنْتَ خَيْرُ واهِبِ

مِنْ شَيْخِ سَوْءٍ يَابِسِ الرَّواجِبِ

مُحَنَّبٍ مِثْلَ الغُرابِ النَّاعِبِ

Umm Khalid Annumairiyya

Nothing is known about the poet other than the poem was written on the death of her son.

1

The morning south wind blew from my son's land his musk, ambergris and lavenderscented presence.

2

I miss him and the thought of him tears my eyes like a prisoner recalling home under the shackles' painful grip, or the cries of a soul away from its love.

أُمُّ خَالد النُّمَيْرِيّة

أَتَتْنَا بِرِيّاتٍ نِصاب هبوبُهَا	اذَا مَا أَتَتْنَا الريَّح مِنْ نَحْوِ أرضِه
وريحٍ خزامي باكرتها جنوبُهَا	أَتَتْنا بمسْكٍ خالطَ المسكَ عنبر
وتنهلُّ عبرات تَفيض غروبُهَا	أحنُّ لذكراهُ اذا مَا ذكرتُهُ
وإعوال نفسٍ غابَ عنها حَبيبُهَا	حنينَ أَسيرٍ نازحٍ شدَّ قَيْدهُ

Ishraqa al-Muharibiyya

Nothing is known about the poet.

1
All lovers wear my castoff clothes and jewels, and gulp down my overspilt drink.

2
I have raced with lovers at love's racetrack and beaten them all at my own pace.

عِشْرَقة المحاربية

جريتُ معَ العُشَّاقِ في حلبةِ الهوى

ففقتُهمُ سبقاً، وجئتُ على رِسلي

فما لبِسَ العشّاقُ من حُللِ الهوى

ولا خَلَعوا إلاّ الثياب التي أُبلي

ولا شربوا كأساً من الحبّ مُرّةُ

ولا حُلوة إلاّ شرابُهُمُ فَضلي

Umm Addahak al-Muharibiyya

Nothing is known about the poet other than she wrote poems about her Dibabi husband with whom she was madly in love.

1
Rider, come and I'll tell you what's burning me.

2
Whatever lovefire people feel, mine's hotter.

3
All I want is to win him over and float in his favour.

أم الضحاك المحاربية

يأيها الراكب الغادي لطِيَّته   عرّج أبثك عن بعض الذي أجدُ

ما عالَج الناسُ من وَجْد تضمّنهم   إلا وجدت به فوق الذي وجَدوا

حسبي رضاه وأنّى في مسرَّتِهِ   ووده آخرَ الأيام أجتهدُ

~⊛~

The contentment of love is hugging, kissing and bellylapping, then hairpulling and bodyrocking that flood the eyes.

شَفَاءُ الحُب تقبيلٌ وضَمٌّ　　وجَرُّ بالبُطون على البطُون

ورهْزٌّ تهمِلُ العَينان مِنه　　واخذُ بالذَّوائب والقُرُون

Anonymous

You don't satisfy a girl with presents and flirting, unless knees bang against knees and his locks into hers with a flushing thrust.

مجهول

لا ينفعُ الجارية اللعابُ
ولا الوشاحان ولا الجلبابُ
من دون ان تلتصق الاركابُ
وتلتقي الاسبابُ والأسبابُ
ويخرج الزُبُّ له لُعابُ

Khansa (d. 646)

Tumadir bint Amr ibn Ashsharid, better known as Khansa, is regarded by classical Arab critics as the finest woman poet. The Prophet Muhammad liked her poetry and used to ask her to recite her poems. Most of her poems are elegies on her two brothers killed in the Jahiliyya and her four sons killed in the Islam wars. She was closely attached to her brother Sakhr, who bailed her and her husband out of financial difficulties.

The Jahilis believed that the blood and the soul are one and the same. When someone was killed the bloodsoul came out of the head of the deceased as an owl called *Hama*, if the deceased was a woman, or *Sada*, if the deceased was a man, and perched on the grave of the deceased screeching, 'Give me a drink! Give me a drink!' until the deceased was avenged. But if the deceased died of natural causes, the *Hama* or the *Sada* would live with the family of the deceased and report news about the family to the deceased for a hundred years. After the *Hamas* and *Sadas* had performed their earthly functions, they flew to paradise where they remained treeperched waiting for their bodyframes to join them. On the Trial Day the dead would rise to be judged to determine who should go to paradise or hell. The unlucky would go to hell to serve their term, at the end of which they would be forgiven and allowed into paradise after having undergone the paradisial cleansing ritual. Once in paradise, the treeperched *Hamas* and *Sadas* would slip back into their former bodyframes to live their new life in paradise.

1
Time is full of surprises.

2
It ignores the tail but lops off the head, it spares the fools but buries and owls the wise.

3
Night and day, though they look different, never change, only people rotaway.

الخنساء

إِنَّ الزَّمانَ وما يَفْنى له عَجَبٌ

أَبْقى لنا ذَنَباً واسْتُوْصِلَ الرَّاسُ

أبقى لنا كل مجهولٍ وفَجَّعَنا

بالحالمينَ فهم هَامٌّ وأرْماسُ

إِنَّ الجديدَيْنِ في طولِ اختلافِهما

لا يفسُدانِ ولكن يفسُد النَّاسُ

~❀~

1

The rising and setting of the sun keep turning on my memory of Sakhr's death.

2

And only the host of mourners crying for their brothers saves me from myself.

يذكَــرني طلوعُ الشمس صخراً
وأذكره لكلّ غروبِ شَمْسٍ

ولولا كثرة الباكين حولي
على إخوانهم لَقَتْلتُ نفْسي

The Islam Period

(622–661)

Fatima bint Muhammad (605–632)

Fatima, the daughter of the Prophet Muhammad, was married at the age of fifteen to her cousin Ali. After a while Ali planned to have a second wife but the Prophet shortshrifted him for entertaining such a thought. Ali also illtreated Fatima and was rebuked by the Prophet. Fatima died five months after the Prophet's death.

The Prophet Muhammad was also known as Ahmad.

Those who smell the soil of Ahmad's grave will have muskscented breath for the rest of their life, but the catastrophes poured on me could night the day.

فاطمة بنت محمد

أن لا يشم مدى الزَّمان غَواليا	ماذا على من شَمَّ تُربة أحمد
صُبَّت على الأيام صرن لياليا	صبت عَلَيَّ مَصَائِبٌ لو أنها

The Mudaris are the descendants of Mudar (fifth century BCE), who is one of the major patriarchs of the northern Arabs from whom the Prophet Muhammad traces his descent.

The Yemenis are the southern Arabs who trace their descent to the Aadi monotheist prophet Hud (4000 BCE).

The Ka'ba was the centre of pilgrimage of the Arabs in the Jahiliyya. It was first built by Adam, then rebuilt by Ibrahim (Abraham) and his son Isma'il (Ishmael). Since the establishment of Islam the Ka'ba has been the centre of pilgrimage for the Muslims.

Muslims regard the Prophet Muhammad as the Last *Rasul* (envoy) of Allah. The Prophet is also known as Rasulullah (Envoy of Allah).

The *Qur'an* is the Muslim Sacred Book Allah revealed to the Prophet Muhammad through the angel Jibreel (Gabriel).

1
The sky turned grey, the sun shot out of sight, leaving a black afternoon.

2
The Prophet is dead, the earth's trembling and depressed over his loss.

3
Let the length and breadth of the land weep for him, let the Mudaris and the Yemenis weep for him, and let the mountains and the Ka'ba weep for him.

4
Favoured Light of Allah and His Last Rasul, may the Qur'an's Lord bless you.

شمس النهار وأظلم العصران	أغبر أفاق السماء وكورت
أسفا عليه كثيرة الرجفان	فالأرض من بعد النبي كئيبة
ولتبكه مضر وكل يمان	فليبكه شرق البلاد وغربها
والبيت ذو الأستار والأركان	وليبكه الطود العظيم جوده
صلى عليك منزل القرآن	يا خاتم الرسل المبارك ضوؤه

~❀~

1

We miss you like the earth longing for rain, and without you we have no more books nor revelations.

2

I wish death had swept us all away before you were buried and mourned.

إنا فقدناك فقد الأرض وابلها

وغاب مذ غبت عنا الوحي والكتب

فليت قبلك كان الموت صادفنا

لما نعيت وحالت دونك الكثب

1
When you were around I used to wander about with you as my wings and shield.

2
But now I bow even to the meek and palmback those who wrong me.

3
The dove that recalls its loss on a branch at night triggers my daily grief.

قد كنتَ ذات حميّةٍ ما عشتَ لي   أمشي البَراحَ وأنتَ كُنْتَ جَناحي

فاليومَ أخضَعُ للضعيفِ وأتَّقي   منه وأدفَعُ ظالمي بالراحِ

وإذا دَعَت قُمريّة شجَناً لها   لَيْلاً على فَنٍ بكَيْتُ صَباحي

Anonymous

The poet went to the Caliph Umar (d. 644) and complained that her husband spent all his time in the mosque. The caliph thought she was praising her husband for his piety and complimented her on keeping her husband on the right path. The poet repeated her complaint again and again, and the caliph repeated his compliments again and again. The poet and judge Ka'b ibn Sawr (d. 656), who happened to be present, said to the caliph that the wife was complaining about her husband neglecting his marital duties. The caliph told Ka'b to deal with the wife's complaint. Ka'b called the woman's husband and said: 'Allah allows you to have four wives, so leave three nights for Allah and one night for your wife.' The caliph said to Ka'b: 'I don't know which is more amazing: your grasp of the wife's complaint or your judgement. Therefore I appoint you Chief Justice of Basra.'

1
Judge of sensible verdicts, the mosque has kept my man away from me.
2
He never sleeps night or day, and as a woman there's nothing I can thank him for.
3
His piety's put him off my bed, so, Ka'b, let's hear your verdict.

مجهول

الهي خليلي عن فراشي مسجدَه	يا أيها القاضي الحكيم رشدَه
فلستُ في حكم النساء احمدَه	نهارهُ وليلُه ما يَرقده
فاقض القضا يا كعبُ لا ترددَه	زَهّده في مضجعي تَعبّده

The Umayyad Period

(661–750)

Laila bint Sa'd al-Aamiriyya (d. 688)

Laila and Majnun (d. 688) are the Arab Romeo and Juliet but without the consummation of their love. Majnun wrote poems about his love for his cousin Laila, which upset her family and made them marry her off to another man. Majnun was brokenhearted and spent the rest of his life in the wild, singing his passionate poems about his lost love.

I have been through what Majnun went through, but he declaimed his love and I treasured mine until it melted me down.

ليلى بنت سعد العامرية

إلاّ وقد كنتُ كما كانَا	لم يكن المجنونُ في حالةٍ
وأنّني قد ذُبْت كِتْمَانا	لكنّه باح بسرٍّ الهوى

Maisun bint Bahdal (d. 700)

Maisun was the wife of the Caliph Mu'awiya and the mother of his son and successor, the Caliph Yazid I (645–683). Maisun was a country girl who hated town life and its trappings.

1
I'd rather be in a lifethrobbing house than in a tall palace.

2
I'd rather have a dog calling lost travellers to my home than a pussycat.

3
I'd rather have a pleasing smock than a chiffon dress.

4
I'd rather have breadcrumbs in my own house than a whole loaf in a palace.

5
I'd rather listen to the winds voicing through wallcracks than to the sound of tambourines.

6
I'd rather be in the company of my proud and finefigured cousin than with the bloated foreign mass.

7
My simple country life appeals to me more than this soft living.

8
All I want is to be in my country home, indeed it is a noble home.

ميسون بنت بَحْدل

أحبُّ إليَّ مِن قَصرٍ مُنيفِ	لَبَيْتٌ تخفِقُ الأرواحُ فيه
أحبُّ إليَّ من قِطٍ أَلوفِ	وكلبٌ يَنبَحُ الطُّرّاق عنّــي
أحبُّ إليَّ من لُبس الشُّفوفِ	ولُبسُ عباءةٍ وتَقَرَّ عيني
أحبُّ إليَّ من أكل الرَّغيفِ	وأكلُ كُسَيْرةٍ في كِسر بيتي
أحبُّ إليَّ من نَقْر الدُّفوفِ	وأصواتُ الرياح بكلّ فَجٍّ
أحبُّ إليَّ من عِلجٍ عَليفِ	وخِرقٌ من بنى عَمِّي نحيفٌ
إلى نفسي من العيش الطَّريفِ	خُشونةُ عِيشتي في البدْو أَشهى
فحَسْبى ذاكَ من وطنٍ شريفِ	فما أبغى سوى وَطني بديلاً

Laila al-Akhyaliyya (d. 706)

Laila was the love of the poet Tawba al-Humaiyyar (d. 699), and was associated with the court of Hajjaj (660–714) whom she admired as a firm and just governor of Iraq and the eastern provinces. On one occasion Hajjaj asked Laila if there was anything serious between Tawba and herself. Laila's answer was that once she thought Tawba hinted his intentions and she told him:

1
Don't tell me what you want, it's beyond your dreams.

2
I have a friend I will not betray, so stick to your mate.

ليلى الأخيلية

فليس إليها ما حَييتَ سبيلُ	وذى حاجةٍ قلنا له لا تَبُحْ بها
وأنت لأخْرَى فارغ وحَلِيلُ	لنا صاحِبٌ لا ينبغي أن نخونَه

～❖～

1

Hajjaj, you are above all men except the caliph and the Forgiving Lord.

2

Hajjaj, you are the shooting star of the exploding war, the people's light that flashes out their darkness.

حَجَّاجُ أنت الذي لا فوقَه أحدُ

إلا الخليفةُ والمُسْتَغْفَرُ الصَّمَدُ

حَجَّاجُ أنت سِنانُ الَحربِ إن نُهِجتْ

وأنت للنَّاسِ في الداجى لنا نَقِدُ

Dahna bint Mas-hal

Dahna was the wife of the poet Ajjaj (d. 708). When Ajjaj failed to consummate the marriage, Dahna complained to the governor that her husband had never touched her since they were married. Ajjaj started embracing and kissing Dahna, and she responded:

1
Lay off, you can't turn me on with a cuddle, a kiss or scent.

2
Only a thrust rocks out my strains until the ring on my toe falls in my sleeve and my blues fly away.

الدهناء بنت مسحل

ولا بتقبيل ولا بشم	تنح لن تملكني بضم
يسقط منه فتخي في كمي	إلا بزعزاع يسلي همـــي

يطير منه حزني وغمـــي

Bint al-Hubab

Nothing is known about the poet.
Aiham Day is a festival held in the Tihama region in the southwest of Arabia.

1

Why should you beat me, husband, when Yahya is windtiring deserts away from me?

2

I wish Yahya would call on me on Aiham Day, then you can whip me as much as you like.

ابنة الحباب

تَنائِفُ لو تَسرى بها الريحُ كَلَّتِ	أُضرَبُ في يَحْيى وبيني وبينه
وإن نَهِلَت مِنيَ السِّياطُ وعلت	ألاَ ليتَ يحى يومَ عَيْهَمَ زارنَا

1

Why are you raving mad, husband, just because I love another man?

2

Go on, whip me, every scar on my body will show the pain I cause you.

أقولُ لعمرو والسِّـياطُ تَلُفُّني

لهنَّ على مَتْنَيَّ شَرُّ دَليلِ

فأشهد يا غيرانُ إنِــي أُحبُّه

بسوْطِكَ فاضرِبْني وأنتَ ذَليلي

Umm al-Ward al-Ajlaniyya

Umm al-Ward was also known as Juml.

1
If you want to know how the old man fared with me, this is what went on.

2
He lolled me the whole night through, and when dawn flashed his private lips thundered rainlessly and his key wilted in my lock.

أم الورد العجلانية

إن تسألوني عنه ما كان الخبر

عذبني الشيخ بأنواع السهر

حتى اذا ما كان في وقت السحر

وركَّب المفتاح في القفل انكسر

ورعدت فقحته بلا مطر

Anonymous

1
My little boy's smell is all lavender.

2
Is every little boy like him, or hasn't anyone given birth before me?

أعرابية

يا حبّذا ريحُ الولدْ   ريحُ الخزامى في البلدْ

أهكذا كلّ ولدْ   أم لم يلد قبلي أحدْ

Anonymous

Arab society preaches what it does not practise. It claims it draws its guidelines from the Qur'an, but the way it lives and behaves does not tally with the message of its source. It is apparent from the Qur'an that polygamy should not be practised, yet society indulges in it.

> You can marry the women you like: two or three or four, but if you feel you cannot be fair to all of them stick to one ... And even if you try to be fair to all the women, you will never succeed, so do not favour one woman with all your affection at the expense of the other woman, but be fair and remember Allah, the Lord of Forgiveness and Love.
>
> *Qur'an: Annisa: 3 & 129*

The poet gave birth to a girl, which upset her polygamous husband who wanted a boy. The husband moved to the nearby house of his other wife. While he was on his way to his other house, the poet saw him and sang the following poem. The husband heard the poem, went to the poet, embraced and kissed her and decided to stay with her and his daughter.

1
Why doesn't Abu Hazm come home instead of staying in the house next door?

2
He's angry it wasn't a boy I bore him, but Allah knows it's not up to me.

3
We only take what's given to us.

أعرابية

ما لأبي حمزة لا يأتينا

يظلّ في البيت الذي يلينا

غضبان ألا نلد البنينا

تالله ما ذلك في أيدينا

وإنما نأخذ ما أُعطينا

Umaima Addumainiyya

Umaima, the wife of the poet Ibn Addumaina (d. 747), was in love with another man who let her down. One night in Medina she saw her love walking with a friend. When her lover left his friend, Umaima sent for the friend and asked him about the identity of her lover. The man told her the identity of his friend and she told him how much she loved his friend. The man promised to bring his friend the following night. On the following night the two men appeared at Umaima's house, and Umaima faced her love and said:

1
You promised me then let me down, so I had to bear the lashing tongues of your haters.

2
You left me a deflecting target so you could remain unscathed.

3
If words could cut through my skin I'd be in shreds.

أُميمة الدمَيثِيَّه

وأنْتَ الذي أخلفْتَني ما وعدتَني   وأشَمتَّ بي مَنْ كان فيكَ يَلُومُ

وأبرزْتَني للناس ثم تركْتَني   لهم غرَضاً أُرْمَى وأنتَ سَليمُ

فلو أنَّ قولاً يَكلُمُ الجِسْمَ قد بَدَا   بجسمِيَ مِن قَولِ الوُشاةِ كُلُومُ

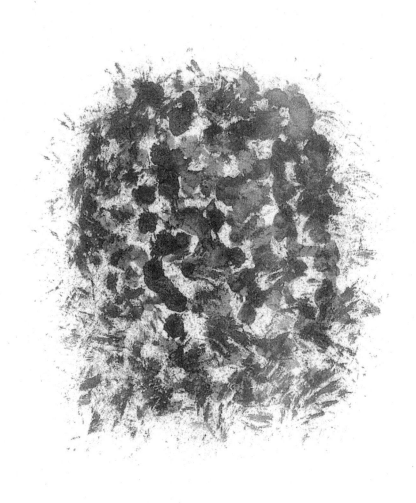

The Abbasid Period

(750–1258)

Hajna bint Nusaib

Hajna was the daughter of the poet Nusaib Assaghir al-Habashi (d. 791). Her father was originally a slave freed by the Caliph Mahdi because he was an impressive poet.

1

Commander of the Faithful, can't you see how the night has covered us with tar?

2

Commander of the Faithful, can't you see we've become beetles run by a beetle boss?

3

Commander of the Faithful, can't you see how poor we are with a poor father?

4

Hardship has drained our strength and there's no one to bail us out, yet the scented pools of the generous caliph are full.

5

Commander of the Faithful, you are the rain that falls on your people.

6

And all those in need come to life through your thoughtful gifts.

الحجناء بنت نصيب

أميرَ المؤمنين ألا ترانا	كأنا من سواد الليل قير
أميرَ المؤمنين ألا ترانا	خنافس بيننا جُعَلٌ كبير
أميرَ المؤمنين ألا ترانا	فقيراتٍ ووالدنا فقير
أضَرَّ بنا شقاء الجَد منه	فليس يَميرُنا فيمن يمير
وأحواض الخليفة مُتْرَعات	لها عَرْف ومَعْروف كبير
أميرَ المؤمنين وأنت غَيْثٌ	يعُم الناسَ وابلُه غزير
يُعاشُ بفضلِ جُودِكَ بعد موتٍ	إذا عالوا وينجبرُ الكسير

Raabi'a al-Adwiyya (714–801)

Raabi'a was born in Basra, Iraq. She was kidnapped as a little girl and sold into slavery. She was later freed on account of her piety, and devoted her life to the worship of Allah. Her exemplary pious life became a model for her sufi successors, and she was venerated as a saint.

1

I put You in my heart to keep me company and leave my body to whoever wants to sit with me.

2

My body is for the entertaining sitter, but the tenant of my heart is my true companion.

رابعة العدوية

إنّي جعلتُك في الفؤاد مُحَدّثي   وأبَحْتُ جسمي من أراد جُلوسي

فالجسم منّي للجليس مؤانِسٌ   وحبيب قلبي في الفؤاد أنيسي

~❀~

1
I love You a double love: I love You passionately and I love You for Yourself.

2
Loving You passionately has put me off others.

3
I love You for Yourself so You would drop Your Shutters to let me see You.

4
I am not the one to be thanked, all thanks must go to You.

أُحِبّكَ حُبّينِ: حبّ الهوى   وحبّاً لأنّك أهلٌ لذاكا

فأمّا الذي هو حبّ الهوى   فشُغْلِي بِذِكْرِك عمّن سواكا

وأما الذي أنت أهلٌ له   فكشفكَ لي الحُجْبَ حتى أراكا

فما الحمدُ في ذا ولا ذاك لي   ولكنْ لك الحمدُ في ذا وذاكا

Laila bint Tarif (d. 815)

Laila was a warrior and the sister of the Khariji leader Walid ibn Tarif (d. 795). The Kharijis formed a sect of uncompromising Muslims who rejected vigorously the assumption of the relatives of the Prophet Muhammad that the caliphate was their preserve. The Kharijis believed the caliphate was open to all Muslims irrespective of their background. When Laila's brother Walid was killed in battle on the hill of Nubatha she cried out:

1
On the hill of Nubatha stood a tomb tall as the tallest mountain, whose guest was a generous soul with an unbent will and a perceptive mind.

2
He was a young man who led a clean life and his wealth was earned by sword and spear.

3
We miss him like the spring, I wish we could have ransomed him with thousands of our nobles.

4
Elder tree, you're still wearing your leaves, don't you miss Ibn Tarif?

5
May Allah shower him with His Salaams, for no lord escapes his fate.

لَيْلى بنت طريف

بنَلَّ نُبَّاثى رسْمُ قبْرٍ كأنَّهُ   على جَبَلٍ فَوْقَ الجِبالِ مُنِيفِ

تَضمَّنَ سَرْواً حَاتِميًّا وسُؤْدَداً   وهمةَ مقدامٍ ورأيَ حصِيف

فتى لا يحبُّ الزاد غلا من التقى   ولا المالَ إلا من قَناً وسيوف

فَقدْناه فِقْدانَ الرَّبيع فليتَنا   فَدَيْناه من سادتنا بألوف

فيا شجرَ الخابور مالك مورقاً   كأنك لم تحزن على ابن طريف

عليك سلامُ الله وقْفاً فإنّني   أرَى الموتَ وقّاعاً بكلّ شَريف

Ulayya bint al-Mahdi (777–825)

Ulayya, the daughter of the Caliph Mahdi, was a poet, singer and composer. Most of her poems were set to music and sung by her. Her mother, a well-known singer and composer from Medina, was the concubine of the Caliph Mahdi. Ulayya's father died when she was a little girl, and she was brought up by her brother the Caliph Harun Arrashid, who was enthralled by her music and singing. Ulayya had several slavelovers whom she mentioned in her poems. Her love affairs were talked about and this prompted the caliph to forbid her to mention the names of her slavelovers. Ulayya bowed to her brother's wish but continued to refer to her slavelovers by using women's names. After a while the caliph lifted the ban. When her brother Harun died Ulayya was grief-stricken and swore never to touch wine or play music again. But her nephew, the new Caliph Amin, persuaded her to break her vow and join him in his musically enlivened drinking parties.

1
Lord, it's not a crime to long for Raib who stokes my heart with love and makes me cry.

2
Lord of the Unknown, I have hidden the name I desire in a poem like a treasure in a pocket.

عُلَيّه بنت المهدي

القلبُ مشتاقٌ إلى ريبِ   يا ربُّ ما هذا من العَيْبِ

قد نَيَّمَتْ قَلْبِي فلَمْ أَسْتطِع   إلا البُكا يا عالِمَ الغَيْبِ

خبَّأْتُ في شِعْرِي اسْمَ الذي   أردتُه كالخَبْءِ في الجَيْبِ

1

I held back my love's name and kept on repeating it to myself.

2

Oh how I long for an empty space to call out the name I love.

كتمتُ اسمَ الحبيب عن العبادِ   وردَّدْت الصبابةَ في فؤادي

فوا شوقي إلى نادٍ خَلِيٍّ   لَعَلِّى باسم من أهوى أنادي

We hint our missives and our eyes are the gobetweens, for letters can be read and contacts let you down.

صحائفُنا إشارتُنا

وأكثرُ رُسْلِنا الحَدَقُ

لأنَّ الكُتْبَ قد تُقرا

وليسَ برسلِنا نَثِقُ

~✷~

My love for Salma havocks my heart with unhealed wounds like shattered glass that can't be smoothed together again.

وفي القلب من وجدٍ بسلمى مع الذي

أرى من توانيها ومن ذَاكَ أعجبُ

جروحٌ دَوامٍ ما تُداوى كلومُها

كما لا أرى كسرَ الزّجاجةِ يُشْعبُ

~❀~

1

Dress the water with wine and knock me back to sleep, and pour a generous flow so you can be the people's imam.

2

May Allah curse the ungiving even if he fasts and prays.

ألْبِسِ الماءَ المداما   وآسقني حتّى أناما

وأفِضْ جودك في الناسِ   تكنْ فيهم إماما

لعنَ اللهُ أخا البخــ   ل وإن صلّى وصاما

~❀~

1
Love thrives on playing hard to get, or else it wears off.

2
A bit of unmixed love is better than a cocktail.

أنصف المعشوق فيه لسَمُج   وضع الحُبُّ على الجَور فلو

لك خير من كثير قد مُزِج   وقليل الحب صِرْفاً خالصاً

Lubana bint Ali ibn al-Mahdi

Lubana was the wife of the Caliph Amin (787–813) and one of the most beautiful women of her times. When her husband was killed before consummating the marriage she cried:

1
Oh hero lying dead in the open, betrayed by his commanders and guards.

2
I cry over you not for the loss of my comfort and companionship, but for your spear, your horse and your dreams.

3
I cry over my lord who widowed me before our wedding night.

لُبَانَة بنت علي بن المهدي

خانتْه قُوَّاده مَع الحرسِ	يا فارساً بالعَرَاء مُطَّرَحاً
بلْ لَلمعالي والرمُح والفَرسِ	أبكيكَ لا للنَّعيم والأنْسِ
أرْمَلَني قبلَ ليلَةِ العُرسِ	أبكي على فارسٍ فُجِعْتُ به

Anonymous

The anthologist and raconteur Asma'i (740–831) entered a country cemetery with a friend and noticed a young woman brightly dressed and jewelled, crying her eyes out over a grave. Asma'i said to his friend: 'Have you ever seen anything stranger than this?' The friend said: 'By Allah, no, nor will I ever see anything like it again.' Asma'i said to the young woman: 'I see you are in mourning but you are not wearing the mourning clothes.' And the young woman said:

1
Grave tenant, my comfort and joy, I've come to visit you clothed and jewelled as though you're still around.

2
I want you to see me as you knew me.

3
Those who watch me weeping for my man ponder the clash of grieving tears with colourful attire.

أعرابية

يا صاحب القبر يا من كان ينعم بي

بالاً ويكثر في الدنيا مواساتي

قد زُرت قبرك في حَلْي وفي حلل

كأنني لست من أهل المصيبات

أردت آتيك فيما كنت تعرفه

أن قد تسر به من بَعْض هيئاتي

فمن رآني رأى عبرى مُولَّهة

عجيبةَ الزيّ تبكي بين أموات

Inan (d. 841)

Inan was the concubine of Annatifi and the friend of the poets Abbas ibn al-Ahnaf (750–809) and Abu Nuwas (762–813). After the death of Annatifi, Inan became the concubine of the Caliph Harun Arrashid. According to the critic and literary biographer Abu al-Faraj al-Isfahani (897–967), Inan was the first significant concubine poet.

1
If my days were in my hands I would have rushed them to my end.

2
There is no goodness around now I've lost you, and I'm crying for my life dragging on.

عِنان

لو في يَدَيّ حسابُ أيامي إذاً   خَطْرفتهُنُ تعجلاً لوفاتي

لا خيرَ بَعْدَكَ في الحياةِ وإنّما   أبكي مخافةَ أنْ تطولَ حياتي

Aasiya al-Baghdadiyya

Aasiya was presented to Abdullah ibn Tahir (798–844), one of the Caliph Ma'mun's generals. After Aasiya spent five days with Ibn Tahir without saying a word, Ibn Tahir asked her: 'Are you dumb? Why don't you speak?' Aasiya replied:

1
They said: Your silence is overstretched.

2
I said: I'm not untongued by fatigue or numbness, but silence is better than quarrelsome talk.

3
They said: You're absolutely right.

4
I said: Show me a cheerful face. Should I unfold a ream of cloth to the unknowing? Or shower the blind with pearls in the dark?

آسِيَة البغداديّة

قالوا: نراكَ تُطيل الصمتَ قلتُ لهم:

ما طولُ صمتي من عِيٍّ ولا خَرَسِ

الصمتُ أحمدُ في الحالين عاقبةً

عندي وأحسنُ بي من منطقٍ شكِسِ

قالوا: فأنت مُصيبٌ لستَ ذا خَطَأً

فقلت: هاتوا أروني وجه مقتَبِسِ

أَنْشُرُ البَزَّ في مَن ليس يعرفه

أم أنثر الدُرَّ بين العُمْي في الغَلَسِ

Zahra al-Kilabiyya

Zahra was in love with Ishaq al-Mawsili (772–850), one of the greatest Abbasid singers and composers.

In her poems Zahra calls Ishaq by the female name of Juml, so her people would not suspect his identity.

1

I keep my passion for Juml to myself.

2

It's burning me up like a sick man's dream of getting well or a mother stricken by the death of her only son or a refugee watching a gathering of friends.

زهَرْاء الكِلابية

وجدي بجمل على أني أجمجمه

وجد السقيم ببرء بعد إدناف

أو وجد ثكلى أصاب الموت واحدها

أو وجد مغترب من بين ألاف

Aa'isha bint al-Mu'tasim

Aa'isha was the daughter of the Caliph Mu'tasim (795–841). When her cousin sent her a poem asking her if she could let him have her maid, as he was in love with her, Aa'isha despatched the maid with the following poem:

1
I read your poem and thought well of you.

2
This beautiful girl is coming to you wearing a darkdispelling glow.

3
So take her contentedly and say no more of what you went through, and don't treat her as a onenight stand like a chance hunter.

عائشة بنت المعتصم

وما أنتَ عندي بالمتهَمَ	قرأتُ كتابَك فيما سألتَ
من النور تجلو سوادَ الظُّلَمْ	أتتك المليحةُ في حُلّةٍ
ولا تشكُ شكوى امرئٍ قد ظُلِمْ	فخذها هنيئاً كما قد سألتَ
كما يفعل الرجلُ المغتنمْ	ولا تحسبنْها لوقتِ المبيتِ

Fadl Ashsha'ira (d. 871)

Fadl was born in Yamama, Bahrain, and brought up in Basra, Iraq. She was sold by her brothers to a leading court secretary, who in turn gave her to the Caliph Mutawakkil (821–861). She became one of the court's entertaining poets. According to the bibliographer Ibn Annadim (d. 1047) she had a diwan of twenty pages.

The following poem was written in response to the poet Abu Dulaf (d. 840) who hinted in a poem that she was not a virgin and he preferred virgins, whom he compared to unpierced pearls.

1
Riding beasts are no joy to ride until they're bridled and mounted.
2
So pearls are useless unless they're pierced and threaded.

فضل الشاعرة

إنْ المطية لا يلذّ ركوبُها   ما لم تذلَّلْ بالزمام وتركبِ

والدُرُّ ليس بنافعٍ اربابَه   حتى يؤلَف للنَّظام بِمثقبِ

Zabba bint Umair ibn al-Muwarriq

Zabba was told if she had married as a young girl she would have known the joys of life. Zabba replied she valued her independence more than men and their wealth and all the treasures of the earth.

In Arab mythology each person has two angels, Yameen and Yasaar. Yameen writes down everything the person's right hand does, and Yasaar writes down everything the left hand does. Then both angels send their reports to Allah.

1
I have been free all my life, and I'm not in debt to any man.

2
I will not be a husband's claim, so shame on the two angels if they don't write: 'It's better to live in hardship than ending up as a whipping girl.'

الزباء بنت عُمَير بن المُورِّق

وليس علي للرجال يدان	أمن بعد أن أُمسي وأُصبح حرة
لبئس إذا ما يكتب الملكان	أصير لزوج مثل مملوكة له
مع العز خير من صروف لسان	لعيش بضر أو بضنك وحاجة

Juml (ninth century)

Juml was the concubine of the poet Idris ibn Abu Hafsa.

1
Juml, if you had been a good Muslim, Allah wouldn't have lumbered you with a youthless pile like Idris, whose spenturge is time's worst joke on you.

2
He comes to you with what you long for, which droops and shrinks as it rendezvous.

3
The unmentionable you desire is now dropless at all times.

جمل

لما ابتليت بشيخ مثل ادريس	يا جُمّل لو كنتِ عند الله مسلمة
أبقى لك الدهر منه شر ملبوس	لما ابتليت بشيخ لا حراك به
عند اللقاء بإدبار وتنكنيس	يلقاك منه الذي تهوين رؤيته
مما تحبين رأساً في المفاليس	أمسى وأصبح مما لا يبوح بِه

Umm Ja'far bint Ali

Nothing is known about the poet.

Leave me alone, you're not my equal, you're not a man of the world nor a man of faith, yet you want to own me, you mindless twit.

أم جعفر بنت علي

فلست لي بقرين	ارجع بغيظك عنا
ولست صاحب دين	ولست صاحب دنيا
واهٍ وحمق حرون	تروم ملكي بعقل

Arib al-Ma'muniyya (797–890)

Arib was born in Baghdad and thought to be the daughter of the vizier Ja'far al-Barmaki. She was sold into slavery at the age of ten after the downfall of her family. She was trained by her master as a poet, singer and composer and became the favourite singer of the Caliph Ma'mun (786–833). She was also a fine chess player.

1
To you treachery is a virtue, you have many faces and ten tongues.

2
I'm surprised my heart still clings to you in spite of what you put me through.

عَرِيب المأمونية

لكم أوجُه شتَى وأْلسِنةٌ عَشْرُ   وأنتم أُناسٌ فيكم الغَدْرُ شيمةٌ

على عظم ما يلقى وليس له صَبْرُ   عَجِبْتُ لقلبي كيف يصبو إليكُمُ

Thawab bint Abdullah al-Hanzaliyya

Nothing is known about the poet other than she was from Hamadan in Iran, and was highly appreciated by the poets and critics Sahib ibn Abbad (938–995) and Tha'alibi (961–1038).

A man asked Thawab to marry him but she ignored him, and as he persisted she wrote to him:

1
Your manhood stretch stands no chance of slipping through my body's niche.

2
So move it away from my body's door and take it back whence it came.

ثواب بنت عبد الله الحنظلية

عند حِري هذا فَرجْ	ايْرُكَ ايْرٌ ما له
وأدخله من حيث خَرَجْ	فاصرفه عن باب حِري

Salma bint al-Qaratisi

The Caliph Muqtafi (1096–1160) heard of Salma's poem and asked: 'See if her description of herself is accurate.' He was told: 'She is even more beautiful.' Muqtafi said: 'Find out about her chastity.' He was told: 'She is the chastest of all people.' Muqtafi then sent her some money so she could look after her art and beauty.

The Thamudis were ancient Arabs who flourished in northern Arabia after the Aadis. The Thamudis spent their summers in palaces in the plains and their winters in houses hewn into the mountains like those of Petra. The Thamudis worshipped seventy gods, which displeased Allah Who sent them the monotheist prophet Salih to show them the right route to Him. The Thamudis mocked Salih for a hundred years, then challenged him to prove his prophethood by a miracle. Salih prayed and Allah responded by sending a shiver through the mountain, and the mountain gave birth to a pregnant shecamel. Salih told the Thamudis to let the shecamel graze freely, and that she would drink water for one day and provide them with milk on the next day. He also warned them that if they killed the shecamel Allah would punish them. The shecamel gave birth, and both camels were killed by the Thamudis. The outraged prophet told the Thamudis that within the next three days their faces would turn yellow, red and black, then they would all die. The Thamudis did not take Salih seriously. But when they saw their faces changing colour, they knew they were doomed. Allah sent the angel Jibreel, who let out a cry which ripped their hearts and burst their ears and killed them instantly. A fire came down from heaven and burnt them. And only Salih and his followers were spared.

1

My eyes outshine the oryx's eyes, my neck outfines the gazelle's neck, and my neckline sparkles my necklaces.

2

I have no problems with my hips, and my breasts don't weigh me down.

3

If I had neighboured the land of Thamud heaven's wrath wouldn't have fallen on the Thamudis.

سلمى بنت القراطيسي

وأجيادُ الظباء فداء جيدي	عيونُ مَها الصريم فداء عيني
لأزينُ للعقودِ من العقود	أزيّنُ بالعقودِ وإن نحري
وتشكو قامتي نقلَ النهود	ولا أشكو من الأوصاب نقلاً
لما نزل العذاب على ثمود	ولو جاورت في بلد ثموداً

Safiyya al-Baghdadiyya (twelfth century)

Nothing is known about the poet.

1
I am the wonder of the world, the ravisher of hearts and minds.

2
Once you've seen my stunning looks, you're a fallen man.

صفية البغدادية

أنا فتنةُ الدُّنيا التي فتَنَتْ حِجَا   كلِّ القُلوبِ فكلُّها في مَغرَمِ

أتَرى مُحيّايَ البديعَ جمالهُ   وتَظُنُّ يا هذا بأنك تَسلَمِ

Taqiyya Umm Ali bint Ghaith ibn Ali al-Armanazi
(1111–1183)

Taqiyya Umm Ali, also known as Sitt Anni'am, was born in Damascus and lived and died in Alexandria. Once she wrote a panegyric for Saladin's nephew Muzaffar in which she gave a detailed description of wine, which prompted Muzaffar to remark that she must have drunk wine in her youth. Taqiyya heard of the remark and sent Muzaffar a martial poem with a note saying that her knowledge of war was like that of wine. She had a small collection of poems.

1
There is nothing good in wine, though a paradisial perk.

2
It ferments the sane, bonkers his mind and instils in him a falling fear.

تقية أم علي

مَذكورةٌ في صفةِ الجنَّهْ	لاَ خيْرَ في الخَمْرِ عَلَى أنَّهَا
خَامَرَهُ في عَقْلِهِ جنَّهْ	لأنَّهَا إنْ خَامَرَتْ عَاقِلاً
فلاَ تَقِى مُهْجَتَهُ جُنَّهْ	يَخَافُ أنْ تَقْذِفَه مِنْ عَلٍ

A pious man, highly regarded by Taqiyya, tripped over in his house and injured his toes. One of the household girls tore off a piece of her scarf and bandaged his injured toes with it. Taqiyya said on the spot:

1
If there was a way to stop your foot bleeding I would have stopped it with my cheek than let the girl use a piece of her scarf.

2
I wish I could kiss the foot that walked along the noble route.

لوْ وجدتُ السبيل جُدْت بَخدِّى   عِوضاً عن خِمارِ تلك الوليدة

كيف لي أن أقَبِّل اليومَ رِجْلاً   سلكت دهرها الطريقَ الحميدة

Shamsa al-Mawsiliyya (thirteenth century)

Shamsa was a highly respected learned poet.

1
She sways in a saffron dress bathed in camphor, ambergris and sandalwood like a narcissus in the garden, a rose in the sun or an image in the temple.

2
She's gracefully slim, and if time tells her, 'Rise,' her hips will say, 'Slow down, no need to rush.'

شَمْسَة المَوْصِلِيّة

وتميسُ بين مُعَصفَرٍ ومزعفرٍ   ومكفَّرٍ ومعنبر ومصندلِ

كَبَهارةٍ في روْضةٍ أو ورْدَةٍ   في جونةٍ أو صورة في هَيْكَلِ

هيفاءُ إن قال الشبابُ لها انهضي   قالت روادفها اقعدي لا تفعلي

The Andalus Period

(711–1492)

Hafsa bint Hamdun (tenth century)

Hafsa was a wit from Wadi al-Hijara (Guadalajara).

1
I have a lover who thinks the world of himself, and when he sees me off he cocks up: 'You couldn't have had a better man.'

2
And I throw back: 'Do you know of a better woman?'

حفصة بنت حمدون

وإذا ما تركته زاد تيها	لي حبيب لا ينثني لعتاب
قلت أيضا وهل ترى لي شبيها	قال لي هل رأيت لي من شبيه

1

Ibn Jamil's view is to see the world in toto, for everyone is taken by his gifts.

2

His manners are like wine with a dash of water, and his looks have grown more handsome since his birth.

3

His sunshine face invites the eye, but his aura keeps people at bay.

رأى ابنُ جميلٍ أن يُرى الدهرَ مجملاً

فكلُّ الورى قد عمهم سَيْبُ نعمتِهْ

لَهُ خُلُقٌ كالخمرِ بَعْدَ امتزاجها

وحُسْنٌ فما أحلاهُ من حين خلقتهْ

بوجهٍ كمثلِ الشمسِ يدعو ببشره

عيُوناً ويعشيها بإفراط هيبتهْ

Aa'isha bint Ahmad al-Qurtubiyya (d. 1010)

Aa'isha was one of the noble ladies of Cordova and a fine calligrapher of the Qur'an. She attended the courts of the Andalusian kings and wrote poems in their honour. She died unmarried.

When one of the poets asked for her hand she scorned him:

1

I am a lioness, and I will never be a man's woman.

2

If I had to choose a mate, why should I say yes to a dog when I'm deaf to lions?

عائشة بنت أحمد القرطبية

أنا لبوة لكنني لا أرتضي   نفسي مناخا طول دهري من أحد

ولوَ أنّني أختارُ ذلك لم أُجب   كلباً وكم غَلّقْتُ سمعي عن أسدْ

Mariam bint Abu Ya'qub Ashshilbi (d. 1020)

Mariam was born in Shilb (Silves), and settled in Seville where she became a highly respected tutor of noble ladies.

1
What is there to hope for in a cobwebbed woman of seventyseven?

2
She babies her way to her stick and staggers like a chained convict.

مريم بنت أبي يعقوب الشِّلْبي

وما يُرتجى من بنتِ سبعينَ حجّةً

وسبعٍ كنسجِ العنكبوت المهلهلِ

تذبُّ دبيبَ الطفلِ تسعى إلى العصا

وتمشي بها مشيَ الأسيرِ المكبّلِ

Umm al-Kiram bint al-Muʿtasim ibn Sumadih (d. 1050)

Umm al-Kiram, the daughter of the king of Almeria, celebrated her love for a wellknown handsome young man by the name of Assummar:

1
I would give my life if we could meet away from spying eyes and eavesdroppers.

2
Oh how I wish my lap could be his home.

أم الكرام بنت المعتصم بن صُمادح

أَلاَ لَيْتَ شِعْرِي هَلْ سَبِيلٌ لِخَلْوَةٍ

يُنَزَّهُ عَنْها سَمْعُ كُلّ مُرَاقِبِ

ويا عَجَباً أَشْتَاقُ خَلْوَةَ مَنْ غَدَا

ومَثْوَاهُ ما بَيْنَ الحَشَا والتَّرائِبِ

~❀~

1

Come and see, folks, what the warmth of love has done.

2

If it hadn't been for him the moon wouldn't have dropped to the ground.

3

I love him, I love him, and wherever he goes my heart follows him.

يا معشرَ الناسِ ألا فاعجبوا   ممّا جَنَتْهُ لوعةُ الحُبِّ

لولاه لم ينزلْ ببدرِ الدجى   من أُفقه العلويً للترب

حسبي بمن أهواهُ، لو أنّهُ   فارَقنَي تابَعَهُ قَلبْي

Umm al-Ala bint Yusuf (d. 1050)

Nothing is known about the poet other than she was from Wadi al-Hijara (Guadalajara).

The poem was written in response to an old man who was in love with the poet.

1
Listen to me, sugar daddy: 'You can't take a girl for a ride.

2
'Don't be like a man who lost his head and sleeps and wakes like a twit.'

أم العلاء بنت يوسف

الشيبُ لا يُخدَعُ فيهِ الصِّبا   بحيلةٍ فاسمعْ إلى نُصحي

فلا تكن أجْهَلَ من في الورى   يبيتُ في الجهلِ كما يُضْحي

~✦~

The dewy reeds in my garden, pennants swaying in the hands of the wind.

لله بُسْتَاني إِذَا

يَهفُو بِهِ الْقَصَبُ الْمُنَدَّى

فَكَأَنَّما كفُّ الرَّيا

ح قَدَ اسْنَدَتْ بَنْداً فَبَنْدَا

If love and song were not spoilt by wine, I'd spend my time drinking glass after glass and get what I long for.

لو لا مُنَافَرةُ المُدا   مةِ للصَّبَابةِ والغِنَا

لعكفتُ بين كئوسها   وجَمَعْتُ أَسْبَابَ المُنَى

―❀―

1
Whatever you do is always good, and our times are graced by your presence.

2
The sight of you is a feast for the eyes, and the mention of your name pleases my ear.

3
Those who haven't met you haven't lived.

وبعلياكم تحلّى الزمنُ	كلُّ ما يصدُر منكم حَسَنُ
وبذكراكم تَلَذُّ الأذنُ	تعطفُ العينُ على منظركم
فهو في نيلِ الأماني يُغْبَنُ	من يعشْ دونكمُ في عمره

Khadija bint Ahmad ibn Kulthum al-Mu'afiri

Khadija, an older contemporary of the poet and critic Ibn Rashiq al-Qairawani (1000–1063), was in love with the poet Abu Marwan. When Khadija's brothers read Abu Marwan's poems on their sister they killed him.

Shaitaan is Satan.

1

They brought us together then ripped us apart with deadly gossip like Shaitaan screwing up people.

2

Abu Marwan, now you're away I can't stop flying out of myself to reach you.

خديجة بنت أحمد بن كُلثوم المُعافرِيّ

جَمعوا بَيننا فلَمّا اجتَمعنا   فَرّقُونا بالزُّورِ والبُهتانِ

ما أرَى فِعلَهم بنا اليومَ إلا   مثلَ فعل الشّيطانِ بالإنسانِ

لَهْفَ نَفسي عليَّ يا لَهْفَ نفسي   منك إنْ بِنْتَ يا أ با مَروانِ

Qasmuna bint Isma'il ibn Yusuf ibn Annaghrila

Qasmuna was the daughter of the influential Jewish poet and vizier Isma'il ibn Yusuf ibn Annaghrila (993–1056), also known as Ibn Naghdala. Among the Jews Ibn Annaghrila was known as Shmuel HaNagid and wrote in both Arabiyya and Hebrew. Qasmuna was once asked by her father to complete a verse he had written:

> I have a cheerful friend who repays kindness
> with ingratitude.

Qasmuna thought for a minute and said:

> Like the moon wearing the sunlight and
> eclipsing the sun.

Her father embraced her and kissed her on her forehead and said: 'With your tenword verse you are a better poet than me.'

When Qasmuna reached nubile age she looked at herself in the mirror and said:

1
I see a garden ripe for picking, but no picker's hand reaching for it.

2
It's painful to watch my youth passing me by, leaving the unmentionable untouched.

قسمونة بنت إسماعيل بن النَّغْرِيلَة

أرى رَوْضَةً قد حان منها قطافُها   ولستُ أرى جانٍ يمدّ لها يدا

فوا أسفا يمضي الشّبابُ مَضيَّعاً   ويبقى الّذي ما إنْ أُسَمِّيهِ مفردا

Qasmuna saw a gazelle grazing in her garden and said:

1
Gazelle, roam and nibble in the everfresh garden, for I'm like you, houri-eyed and alone.

2
Both of us are lost without our dates, so let's take our fate in our stride.

يا ظَبْية ترعى بروضٍ دائماً   إنّي حكيتُكِ في التوحّشِ والحوَرْ

أمسى كلانا مفرداً عن صاحبٍ   فلنصطبر أبداً على حكم القدرْ

Ghassaniyya al-Bajjaniyya (eleventh century)

Nothing is known about the poet other than she was from Bajjana (Pechina).

1
I knew him when life was smooth under the shadow of his love whose garden was an eyeful of green.

2
Those were happy nights, when love was guiltless with no fear of breaking up.

الغسَّانية البجانية

عَهِدْتُهُمُ والعيشُ في ظلً وَصلِهِم
أنيق وروضُ الوَصلِ أخضَر فَينانُ

لياليَ سعدٍ لا يُخَافُ على الهوى
عتابٌ ولا يُخْشَى عل الوصل هجرانُ

Wallada bint al-Mustakfi (d. 1091)

Wallada, the daughter of the Umayyad Caliph Mustakfi (976–1025), was the object of passion of the poet Ibn Zaidun (1004–1071). Ibn Zaidun was imprisoned for his attempt to overthrow the Cordovan regime, and Wallada's love for him wore off, though he never stopped loving her and wrote for her passionate poems that have continued to reverberate to this day. Wallada was a trendsetter and a very beautiful woman.

Wallada wrote the first verse of the following poem on the righthand side of the front of her robe, and the second verse on the lefthand side.

1
By Allah, I'm made for higher goals and I walk with grace and style.

2
I blow kisses to anyone but reserve my cheeks for my man.

وَلَّادَة بنت المستكفي

أنا واللهِ أصلحُ للمعالي   وأمشي مشيتي وأتيهُ تِيها

وأُمْكِنُ عاشقي من صَحْن خدي   وأُعطي قبلتي مَنْ يشتَهيها

~❀~

1
Come and see me at nightfall, the night will keep our secret.

2
When I'm with you I wish the sun and moon never turn up and the stars stay put.

ترقَّبْ إذا جَنَّ الظَّلامُ زيارتي

فإنّي رأيتُ الليلَ أكتمَ للسرِّ

وبي منك ما لو كان بالشمس لم تلحْ

وبالبدرِ لم يطلعْ وبالنجمِ لم يَسْرِ

1

If you were faithful to our love you wouldn't have lost your head over my maid.

2

You dropped a branch in full bloom for a lifeless twig.

3

You know I am the moon yet you fell for a tiddly star.

لو كنتَ تُنْصِفُ في الهوى ما بيننا

لم تهوَ جاريتي ولم تتخيَّرِ

وتركت غُصناً مثمراً بجمَاله

وجنحتَ للغصنِ الذي لم يُثمرِ

ولقَدْ علمتَ بأنني بدرُ السما

لكن ولعتَ لشقوتي بالمشتري

~❀~

1
Ibn Zaidun, in spite of his qualities, is unkind to me for no reason.

2
He looks at me menacingly as if I'd come to unman his boyfriend Ali.

إنَّ ابن زيدون على فضلِهِ   يغتابني ظلماً ولا ذنب لي

يلحظني شزراً إذا جئتُه   كأنَّني جئتُ لأخصي علي

$\sim\!\circledast\!\sim$

1

Ibn Zaidun, though a man of quality, loves the unbent rods in men's trousers.

2

If he saw a joystick dangling from a palm tree he'd fly after it like a craving bird.

إنَّ ابنَ زيدون على فضلهِ   يعشقُ قُضبَان السراويلِ

لو أبْصرَ الأيرَ على نخلةٍ   صارَ من الطير الأبابيلِ

1

Is there a way we can meet and share our love once more?

2

In the winter I used to wait on hot coals for your visits.

3

Now I feel worse since you've gone and confirmed my fears.

4

The nights roll on, but absence stays and patience won't free me from longing's grip.

5

I hope Allah waters the new land that's become your home.

ألا هَلْ لنَا من بعد هذا التفرقِ

سبيلٌ فيشكو كلُ صبّ بما لقي

وقد كنتُ أوقاتَ التزاور في الشتّا

أبيتُ على جمرٍ من الشوق محرقِ

فكيف وقد أمسيتُ في حالِ قطعةٍ

لقد عَجِلَ المقْدُورُ ما كنتُ أتَّقي

تمُرُّ الليالي لا أرى البينَ ينقضي

ولا الصبرَ من رقِّ التشوق معتقي

سقى اللهُ أرضاً قَدْ غدتْ لكَ منزلاً

بكل سَكُوبٍ هاطلِ الوبل مُغْدِقِ

I'timad Arrumaikiyya (1041–1095)

In 1059 the governor of Shilb (Silves), Prince Muhammad ibn Abbad, was visiting Seville. One day Prince Muhammad was walking along the banks of the Guadalquivir with his adviser and confidant the Shilban poet Ibn Ammar (1031–1085). The prince stopped and improvised the first line of a couplet:

The wind rippled a mailcoat in the water

and suggested to Ibn Ammar to complete the couplet. Ibn Ammar went blank, and out of the blue a girl who was washing clothes by the river said:

What a shield it would make if it froze.

The prince was impressed by the verse, and turning around, was surprised to see the author of the verse was a beautiful girl. The prince asked the girl her name and if she was married, and she said her name was I'timad, she was single and her master was Arrumaik ibn Hajjaj. The prince bought the girl and married her in Shilb. The prince was nineteen and I'timad was eighteen. The prince adopted the title of Mu'tamid which is based on his wife's name. In 1069 Mu'tamid succeeded his father as king of Seville whose domain stretched from Cordova in Spain to Silves in Portugal. Once I'timad saw men treading on mud, and told Mu'tamid she would like to walk on mud like them. Mu'tamid made a muddy pile of musk and camphor soaked in perfumes for her to walk on. On another occasion snow fell unexpectedly and she told Mu'tamid she would like to see the snow again. Mu'tamid planted almond trees on the hills overlooking the town, and every spring I'timad watched from the window of her room the hills covered in almond blossom white as snow. Eventually Mu'tamid was overthrown by the Almoravid Sultan Yusuf ibn Tashifin (1019–1106) and imprisoned in Aghmat near Marrakesh. I'timad stayed close to him and died a few days before him.

While Mu'tamid was outside Seville, he sent I'timad a note asking if she would like to join him or would rather have him join her. I'timad wrote back:

I urge you to come faster than the wind to mount my breast and firmly dig and plough my body, and don't let go until you've flushed me thrice.

أعتماد الرميكية

بخطى تسبق الرياح حثاثِ	غرضي أن يكون منك وصولٌ
بعَمود يخط كالمحراثِ	ثمّ تعلو صَدري وتحرث بَطني
لم تدعني إلى بلوغ الثلاثِ	وإذا ما حصلت للنيك فوقي

Muhja bint Attayyani al-Qurtubiyya (d. 1097)

Muhja, the daughter of a figseller, was a protégée of Wallada and one of the most beautiful ladies of her times. As Muhja's relationship with Wallada became strained she lashed out against Wallada.

According to the Qur'an, Mariam (Mary) gave birth to Isa (Jesus) under a palm tree.

1
I thought your name is Wallada and not the mother of fatherless children.

2
Mariam's refuge is a palm tree, but yours a standing invitation.

مهجة بنت التياني القرطبية

من غيرِ بعل فُضِحَ الكاتمُ	ولادةٌ قد صرتِ ولادةً
نخلةُ هذي ذَكرٌ قائمُ	حَكَتْ لنا مريَمَ لكنّهُ

Nazhun al-Gharnatiyya (d. 1100)

Nazhun was exceptionally beautiful, wellread in poetry and a notorious wit. She was the love of the vizier Abu Bakr ibn Sa'id who wrote her a note in which he referred to her many men friends, and she responded:

1
I put you up, Abu Bakr, in a place beyond the reach of other men.

2
Isn't my breast your loving home?

3
Although I have many lovers you're still top of the list.

نزهون الغرْناطية

حللتَ أبا بكر محلاً منعتُهُ

سواكَ وهل غيرُ الحبيب له صدري

وإن كانَ لي كم من حبيبٍ فإنّما

يُقدّمُ أهلُ الحقّ حُبَّ أبي بكرِ

1

Bless those wonderful nights, and best of all Saturdays.

2

If you had been there you'd have seen us locked together under the chaperone's sleepful eyes like the sun in the arms of the moon or a panting gazelle in the clasp of a lion.

لله درُّ اللّيالي ما أحيسنها

وما أُحيسن منها ليلةَ الأَحَدِ

لو كنتَ حاضرنا فيها وقَدْ غفلتْ

عينُ الرقيب فلمْ تنظرْ إلى أحدِ

أبصرتَ شمسَ الضُّحَى في ساعدي قمرٍ

بل رِيَم خازمةٍ في ساعَدَيْ أسدِ

Amat al-Aziz (twelfth century)

Nothing is known about the poet other than she was the paternal greataunt of the Andalusian literary biographer and historian Ibn Dihya (1150–1235) who was the author of *Al-Mutrib min Ash'aar al-Maghrib* (*Entertaining Poems from the West*).

1
Your eyes thrill my body, my eyes thrill your cheeks.

2
A thrill for a thrill, an equal score, so why this coldness?

أمة العزيز

ولحظنا يجرحكم في الخدود	لحاظُكُم تجرحنا في الحشا
فما الذي أوجب هذا الصدود	جُرح بجُرح فاجعلوا ذا بذا

Buthaina bint al-Mu'tamid ibn Abbad (1070–?)

Buthaina was the daughter of Mu'tamid and I'timad Arrumikiyya, the king and queen of Seville. After her father was overthrown she was sold into slavery. She was bought by a man who gave her to his son as a concubine. She revealed her identity to the son and told him she would not let him touch her unless he married her. The son agreed to marry her. Buthaina wrote the following poem and sent it to her father who gave her his blessing.

1
Listen to my words, echoes of noble breeding.

2
You cannot deny I was snatched as a spoil of war, I, the daughter of a Banu Abbad king, a great king whose days were soured by time and chased away.

3
When Allah willed to break us hypocrisy fed us grief and ripped us apart.

4
I escaped but was ambushed and sold as a slave to a man who saved my innocence so I could marry his kind and honourable son.

5
And now, father, would you tell me if he should be my spouse, and I hope royal Rumaika would bless our happiness.

بثينة بنت المعتمد بن عباد

فهي السلوك بدت من الأجياد	اسمع كلامي واستمع لمقالتي
بنت لملك من بني عباد	لا تنكروا أني سبيت وأنني
وكذا الزمان يؤول للإفساد	ملك عظيم قد تولى عصره
وأذاقنا طعم الأسى عن زاد	لما أراد الله فرقة شملنا
فدنا الفراق ولم يكن بمراد	قام النفاق على أبي في ملكه
لم يأت في إعجاله بسداد	فخرجت هاربة فحازني امرؤ
من صانني إلا من الانكاد	إذ باعني بيع العبيد فضمني
حسن الخلائق من بني الأنجاد	وأرادني لنكاح نجل طاهر

ومضى إليك يسوم رأيك في الرضى

ولأنت تنظر في طريق رشادي

إن كان ممن يرتجى لوداد	فعساك يا أبتي تعرفني به
تدعو لنا باليمن والإسعاد	وعسى رميكية الملوك بفضلها

Hind (twelfth century)

Hind was a lutenist. The vizier Aamir ibn Yannaq (d. 1152) invited Hind to visit him with her lute, she replied:

Noble Lord, proud line of the highest rank, I'll quickly come to you as my reply with your messenger.

هند

شُمَّ الأُنوفِ من الطراز الأوَّلِ	يا سيداً حاز العُلى عن سادةٍ
كنتُ الجواب مع الرسول المُقبل	حسبي من الإسراعِ نحوكَ أنّني

Umm al-Hana bint Abdulhaqq ibn Atiyya
(twelfth century)

Umm al-Hana was the daughter of the wellknown Cordovan poet and judge Ibn Atiyya (1088–1148). She was a quickwitted and learned poet and wrote a book on graves. Her father was appointed chief justice of Almeria, and he came home with tearful eyes feeling sorry for having to leave his home town, Cordova. Umm al-Hana saw the state he was in and improvised the following poem:

1
My love wrote he's homing to me, joy made me cry.

2
My eyes, happy or sad, your tears roll on.

3
Flash and smile on the day of his coming, and leave the tears for the night of parting.

أم الهناء بنت عبد الحق بن عطية

جاء الكتاب من الحبيب بأنه

سيزورني فاستعبرت أجفاني

غلب السرور علي حتى أنه

من عظم فرط مسرتي أبكاني

يا عين صار الدمع عندك عادة

تبكين في فرح وفي أحزان

فاستقبلي بالبشر يوم لقائه

ودعي الدموع لليلة الهجران

Hafsa bint al-Hajj Arrakuniyya (d. 1190)

Hafsa was a noble lady from Granada who was in love with the vizier and poet Abu Ja'far ibn Sa'íd. They met regularly and wrote poems about their love affair. The king was also in love with Hafsa, but he failed to win her affection and killed Abu Ja'far, hoping he would have no rivals. Hafsa was brokenhearted, and withdrew to Marrakesh where she became the tutor of the families of the Almohad Sultans Abdulmu'min ibn Ali al-Kumi (1094–1163), Yusuf ibn Abdulmu'min (1138–1184) and Ya'qub al-Mansur ibn Yusuf (1160–1199) until she died.

1
Ask the lightning when it roarrips the nightcalm if it's seen my man as it makes me think of him.

2
By Allah, it shakes my heart and turns my eyes into a raining sky.

حفصة بنت الحاج الركونية

سلوا البارقَ الخفّاقَ والليلُ ساكنٌ   أظلَّ بأحبابي يذكِّرني وَهْنا

لعمري لقد أهدى لقلبيَ خفقةً   وأمطرني مُنْهَلٌّ عارضِهِ الجفنا

~✲~

1

I'm jealous of my chaperone's eyes and of the time and place that claim you.

2

If I keep you in my eyes until the world blows up I'd still want you more.

أغارُ عليك من عَيْنيْ رقيبي   ومنك ومن زمانك والمكانِ

ولو أنيّ خبأتُك في عيوني   إلى يومِ القيامةِ ما كفاني

1

I know too well those marvellous lips.

2

By Allah, I'm not lying if I say I love sipping their finerthanwine delicious dew.

ثنائي على تلكَ الثّنايا لأنّني   أقول على علم وأنطق عن خُبْرِ

وأُنصفها لا أكذبُ الله إنّني   رشْفتُ بها ريقاً أرقَّ مِنَ الخمرِ

Hafsa called at Abu Ja'far's house and handed the porter the following poem to be given to Abu Ja'far. As soon as Abu Ja'far read the poem he said: 'This can only be Hafsa.' So Abu Ja'far went to receive Hafsa but she had already gone.

1
The girl with the gazelle neck is here and longs to meet you.

2
I wonder if she'll be graced with a welcome or told you're indisposed?

زائر قد أتى بجيدِ غزال   طامع من مُحبه بالوصال

أتراكم بإذْنكم مُسْعِفيه   أم لكم شاغلٌ من الأشغال

~✦~

1

If you were not a star I would be in the dark.

2

Salaam to your beauty from one who misses the thrills of your company.

ولو لَمْ يكن نجماً لما كانَ ناظري   وقد غبتُ عنهُ مُظلماً بعد نورِهِ

سلامٌ على تلك المحاسنِ من شَجٍ   تناءت بنعماه وطيبِ سرورِهِ

≈✦≈

I send my earthrilling poems to visit you like a garden that can't go visiting but reaches out with its floating scent.

سار شعري لك عنّى زائراً   فأعِرْ سَمْعَ المعالى شِنْفَهُ

وكذاك الروضُ إذْ لم يَسْتطعْ   زَورةً أَرْسَلَ عنه عَرْفَهُ

After Hafsa had spent the night with Abu Ja'far in his garden, he sent her a poem telling her how pleased were the garden, the birds, the river and the breeze with the way they had spent their night. Hafsa wrote back:

1
When we walked along the garden path, there was no smile on the garden's face but green envy and yellow bile.

2
And when we stood on the riverbank, the river was not a bubble of rippling joy, and the dove cooed with spite.

3
You shouldn't take the world as it looks just because you're good.

4
Even the sky blazed on its stars to scan our love.

لعمرُكَ ما سُرَّ الرياضُ بوصلنا   ولكنّهُ أبدى لنا الغلَّ والحسدْ

ولا صفَّقَ النهرُ ارتياحاً لقربنا   ولا غَرَّدَ القُمْرِيُّ إلاَّ لما وجدْ

فلا تحسنِ الظنَّ الذي أنتَ أهلهُ   فما هو في كلَّ المواطن بالرَّشَدْ

فما خلتُ هذا الأفقَ أبدى نجومه   لأمرٍ سوى كيما تكونَ لنَا رصَدْ

Hafsa wrote the following poem to Abu Ja'far asking him if they could meet. He answered with a poem in which he said: 'It is not the garden that goes visiting but the pleasant breeze should visit the garden.'

Jamil (d. 701) and Buthaina (d. 701) were cousins who fell in love with each other but were forbidden to marry because Jamil had aired his love for Buthaina in his poems. Buthaina was married off to another man, but Jamil did not stop writing love poems for her. Jamil and Buthaina met every now and then in secret until their last days.

1
Shall I call on you or will you come to me?

2
I'm always yours whenever you want me.

3
When you break at noon you'll need a drink and you'll find my mouth a bubbling spring and my hair a refuge shade.

4
So be quick with your reply as it's not nice of Jamil to keep Buthaina waiting.

أزوركَ أم تزورُ فإنَّ قلبي إلى ما تشتهي أبداً يميلُ

فثَغري موردٌ عذبٌ زلالٌ وفَرْعُ ذُؤَابتي ظِلٌّ ظَليلُ

وقد أمَّلتُ أن تظما وتَضحَى إذا وافى إليكَ بيَ المقيلُ

فَعَجل بالجوابِ فما جميلٌ أناتُك عن بُثينةَ يا جميلُ

≈❋≈

1

I send salaams that charm the petals to life and stir the doves to sing in their branches.

2

Though out of my sight you permanent my heart.

3

You shouldn't think your woman will blot you out of her mind because you're out of reach.

4

For as long as I'm around, by Allah, nothing of the kind will happen.

سلامٌ يفتـــحُ في زهرةِ الـــ   كمامَ ويُنْطِقُ وُرقَ الغصونْ

على نازح قد ثَوَى في الحَشا   وإن كان تحرمَ منهُ الجفونْ

فلا تحسبوا البُعدَ يُنسيكمُ   فذلكَ واللهِ ما لا يَكونْ

As soon as Hafsa heard of the murder of Abu Ja'far she wore her mourning clothes and grieved openly for him. Hafsa was threatened for mourning Abu Ja'far, and she cried out:

1
They killed my love then threatened me for wearing my mourning clothes.

2
Let Allah bless those who grieve or untap their tears for the man killed by his haters.

3
Let the morning clouds, like his generous hand, shower the earth that blankets him.

هدَّدوني من أجل لِبُس الحِداد   لحبيبٍ أرْدُوه لى بالحِداد

رحم الله من يجودُ بدمع   أو يَنُوح على قتيلِ الأعاد

وسقَّتْه بمثل جُود يديه   حيث أضْحَى من البلاد الغَواد

Ashshilbiyya (twelfth century)

Nothing is known about Ashshilbiyya, not even her name, other than she was from Shilb (Silves) in southern Portugal. The poem is a plea to the Almohad Sultan Ya'qub al-Mansur (1160–1199), who repossessed Shilb from the Portuguese in 1191, to save Shilb from the excesses of the governor and the tax collectors.

1
It's time for the proud eyes to cry, even the stones are weeping.

2
When you go to town seek the Merciful's hand to keep you from harm.

3
Tell the emir when you reach his door: 'Shepherd, your flocks are dying and have nowhere to graze. You left them as prey for the raiding beasts.'

4
Shilb, yes, Shilb was paradise before the tyrants, scornful of Allah's wrath, looted and furnaced it, but nothing escapes Allah.

الشلبية

ولقد أرَى أنَّ الحجارة باكيةْ	قد آنَ أنْ تبكي العُيونُ الآبيةْ
إن قَدَّرَ الرحمنُ رَفْعَ كراهيه	يا قاصدَ المصر الذي يُرجَى بهِ
يا راعياً إنّ الرعيّةَ فانيه	نادِ الأميرَ إذا وقفت ببابهِ
وتركتها نهبَ السباع العاديه	أرسَلتْهَا هَمَلاً ولا مَرْعًى لها
فأعادها الطاغون ناراً حاميه	شِلِبٌ كلا شلبٍ وكانت جنّةً
واللهُ لا تخفى عَلَيَه خافيه	حافوا وما خافوا عقوبةَ ربهم

Aa'isha al-Iskandaraniyya

Aa'isha was also known as Zahrat al-Adab (Flower of Literature), and had a literary salon called Arrawd (The Garden). One of her salon frequenters sent her a poem in which he said his heart was crackling on live coals because of her. She responded:

If your heart is a furnace don't spark out its secrets, for I fear it'll fire up the garden and its flowers.

عائشة الإسكندرانية

فلا تَبْعَثَنَّ بأسراره	إذا كان قلبُك ذا جاحم
على الروضِ أو بعض أزهاره	فإني لأُشْفِقُ من ناره

Hamda bint Ziyad (d. 1204)

Hamda was from Wadi Aash (Guadix) near Granada, and was known as the Khansa of Andalus. One day she was walking with her friends along the river, which branched into several streams, and then she swam in the river playfully.

1
My tears bare my secrets in a river of apparent charm.

2
Rivers touring gardens and gardens touring rivers.

3
And among the gazelles is a joy doe who's palmed my heart and unsleeped my eyes.

4
And when she unpins her hair you see the moon in a dark horizon, as though the dawn has lost a brother and worn his mourning dress.

حمدة بنت زياد

لهُ للحسن آثارٌ بوَادي	أباحَ الدمعُ أسراري بوَادي
ومن روض يَطُوفُ بكل وادي	فمن نهرٍ يطوفُ بكلّ روضٍ
لها لبي وقد ملكَتْ فؤادي	ومن بينِ الظّباء مهاةُ إنْسٍ
وذاكَ الأمْرُ يَمْنعُني رقادي	لها لَحْظٌ تُرقّده لأمْرٍ
رأيتَ البدرَ في أفق السواد	إذا سدلَتْ ذوائبها عَلَيْها
فمن حزنٍ تَسَرْبَلَ بالحداد	كأنَّ الصّبحَ ماتَ لهُ شقيق

1

The tonguestingers want to split us up, though we've done them no harm.

2

They deafen us with their gossip and no one can unmouth them.

3

So we stormed them with your eyes and my tears, and finished them off with sword, fire and flood.

ولمّا أبى الواشونَ إلّا فراقَنا   وما لهمُ عندي وعندكَ من ثارِ

وشَنّوا على أسماعنا كلَّ غارةٍ   وقَلَّ حُمَاتي عند ذاك وأنصاري

غزوتهمُ من مقلتيكَ وأدْمعي   ومن نفَسي بالسيفِ والسَيْلِ والنارِ

Umm Assa'd bint Isam al-Himyari (d. 1243)

Umm Assa'd, also known as Sa'duna, was from Cordova.

Sculptures and paintings of the Prophet Muhammad's shoes were in circulation in Andalus at the time of Umm Assa'd.

The Tooba Tree is a scented tree in paradise, which produces pure honey-sweet gum.

Salsabeel is a spring in paradise.

1
I will kiss the Prophet's sculpted shoes if I cannot have the originals so I may kiss him in paradise under the Tooba Tree and drink contentedly cupfuls of Salsabeel to cool down the holocaust within my ribs.

2
Lovers of all times hang on to the memory of those they love.

أم السعد بنت عصام الحميري

للثم نعلِ المصطفى من سبيلْ	سألتُ التمثالَ إذ لَمْ أجدْ
في جنةِ الفردوسِ أسنى مقيلْ	لعلَّني أحظى بتقبيلهِ
أُسقى بأكواسٍ من السلسبيلْ	في ظلّ طُوبى ساكناً آمناً
يسكنُ ما جاش بهِ من غليلْ	وأمسحُ القلبَ به عَلّهُ
يهواه أهلُ الحبّ في كل جيلْ	فطالما استشفى بأطلالٍ مَنْ

Victims of a Map: A Bilingual Anthology of Arabic Poetry

Edited by Abdullah al-Udhari

'An excellent collection of verses from three of the most modern Arab poets.' *International Journal of Islamic and Arabic Studies*

Victims of a Map presents some of Mahmud Darwish, Samih al-Qasim and Adonis's finest work in translation, alongside the original Arabic, including thirteen poems by Darwish never before published – in English or Arabic – and a long work by Adonis written during the 1982 siege of Beirut, also published here for the first time.

'A five-star publication ... I would like to see it widely bought, read, and discussed in the English-speaking world.' *Orbis*

'A beautifully produced little book.' *Middle East International*

'A very useful introduction to modern Arabic poetry ... an elegant, precise translation.' *Al-Majalla*

Literature • 978-0-86356-524-3 • £9.99 / $14.95

Desert Songs of the Night: 1,500 years of Arabic Literature

Edited by Suheil Bushrui and James M. Malarkey

'An arresting collection ... Dipping into this enchanting anthology one is struck by the sheer variety of voices that have emerged from the Arab world' *Daily Telegraph* ****

Compiled by two leading scholars of Arabic Literature, *Desert Songs of the Night* is an extraordinary collection of some of the finest poetry and prose by Arab writers over the past 1,500 years.

From the mystical imagery of the Qur'an and the colourful stories of *The Thousand and One Nights*, to the powerful verses of longing of Mahmoud Darwish and Nazik al-Mala'ika, this captivating collection includes translated excerpts of works by the major authors of the period, as well as by lesser known writers of equal significance.

Desert Songs of the Night showcases the vibrant and distinctive literary heritage of the Arabs. Beautifully produced, this is the ideal book for lovers of world literature and for those who seek an acquaintance with gems of Arab thought and expression.

'A wonderful introduction to fifteen centuries of a literature still largely unknown in the West ... Absolutely essential reading for our troubled times.' Alberto Manguel

'This remarkable anthology spans 1,500 years of Arab literary genius' Hanan al-Shaykh

Literature • 978-0-86356-175-7 • £12.99 / $18.95

Modern Arabic Short Stories: A Bilingual Reader

Edited by Ronak Husni and Daniel N. Newman

The twelve stories collected here are by leading authors of the short story form in the Middle East today. In addition to works by writers already well-known in the West such as Idwār al-Kharrāt, Fuʾād al-Takarlī and Nobel Prize-winning Najīb Mahfūz , the collection includes stories by key authors whose fame has hitherto been restricted to the Middle East. Ideal for students of Arabic as well as lovers of literature who wish to broaden their appreciation of the work of Middle Eastern writers.

Literature • 978-0-86356-436-9 • £14.99 / $21.95

A Reader of Modern Arabic Short Stories

Edited by Sabry Hafez and Catherine Cobham

This reader consists of the full Arabic texts of eleven short stories by established Egyptian, Iraqi, Syrian and Jordanian writers. Each story is supplemented by an introduction, with biographical information about the author, placing him in his literary context; a description of the contents; and a brief analysis of the story itself, in English.

'Excellent ... the analytical introductions to each story are not only accurate but full of critical insight.'
Roger Allen, *Journal of Semitic Studies, Oxford Journals*

Literature • 978-0-86356-436-9 • £14.99 / $21.95